I0439684

BLM Technical Note 433

An Assessment of the Effects of Oil and Gas Field Activities on Nesting Raptors in the Rawlins, Wyoming and Price, Utah Field Offices of the Bureau of Land Management

Jeff P. Smith, Steven J. Slater[1], and Mike C. Neal

HawkWatch International, Inc.
2240 South 900 East
Salt Lake City, Utah 84106

[1] Phone: (801) 484-6808 x108
Email: sslater@hawkwatch.org

Prepared for:
U.S. Department of Interior,
Bureau of Land Management
Utah State Office, Salt Lake City,
Wyoming State Office, Cheyenne, and
Colorado State Office, Lakewood

Table of Contents

List of Tables

List of Figures

Introduction

Approximately 15 million ha of land managed by the Bureau of Land Management (BLM) in the western United States are leased for oil, gas, or geothermal energy production, but few studies have specifically investigated the potential disturbance effects energy development may have on nesting raptors. The potential for disturbance is suggested by studies of nesting raptors and other human activities, such as construction, hiking, camping, and rock climbing. The potential for nest disturbance is influenced by factors such as disturbance proximity and type, as well as previous exposure to disturbance.

Federal legislation, specifically the Migratory Bird Treaty Act and Bald and Golden Eagle Protection Act (BGEPA), prohibit the "taking" of raptors, their young, or nests. Additionally, the BGEPA protects nesting eagles from human disturbance. As a result, federal land management plans commonly include spatial and/or temporal nest-protection stipulations that restrict human activities near raptor nests to ensure compliance with federal legislation. Specific stipulations applied by land managers typically are based on limited data on nest disturbance collected for some of the more abundant or visible raptor species found within the relevant area of responsibility. Because of these limited and often sporadic datasets, proactive stipulations applied to nesting raptors often vary between and within federal agencies.

In 2006, the BLM entered into an assistance agreement (JSA065003) with HawkWatch International, Inc. to conduct a two-phase "Raptor Radii Research Project." The underlying goal of this research was to assess existing protective spatial and temporal buffers and provide guidance to minimize potential disturbance to nesting raptors exposed to oil and gas (OG) development activities. Phase I of the project was intended to be a retrospective evaluation of past raptor nesting activity in relation to concurrent OG development activity on lands managed primarily by the Price, Utah, and Rawlins, Wyoming, Field Offices of the BLM. Phase II was intended to be a two-year field study designed to experimentally test raptor nest-disturbance thresholds in Colorado, Utah, and Wyoming study areas selected based on current and expected OG development activities and available raptor nesting data. This report provides the results of the Phase I portion of the Raptor Radii Research Project.

The major goals of Phase I of the Raptor Radii Research Project were:

Goal 1.   Compile historic data to evaluate the relationship between past OG development activities and nesting raptors.

Goal 2.   Where suited, use historic data to evaluate the effectiveness of previously applied raptor nest-protection buffers.

Goal 3.   Assess strengths and weaknesses of historic data and provide recommendations for improvement.

We address the first two goals in this technical note and third goal in a separate document (Smith et al. 2010). To achieve the first two goals, we established the following objectives:

Objective 1.   Describe temporal trends in development near focal-species nest clusters.

Objective 2.   Describe distributional patterns of nest-cluster status in relation to development hotspots.

Objective 3.   Assess relationships between nest-cluster status and development.

Objective 4.   Assess Ferruginous Hawk (*Buteo regalis*) nest success and productivity in relation to development in the Rawlins, Wyoming study area.

Objective 5.   Assess the response of Ferruginous Hawks to artificial nest structures (ANSs) in the Rawlins, Wyoming study area.

Methods

We adopted a "nest-cluster" approach for Phase I assessments of data collected in the Price, Utah, and Rawlins, Wyoming, study areas. The Price study area topography was dominated by canyons and cliffs and primarily contained pinyon-juniper (*Pinus edulis-Juniperus* spp.) vegetation, interspersed with sagebrush (*Artemisia* spp.) and grass openings. The Utah Division of Wildlife Resources (UDWR) began conducting annual helicopter surveys in the Price study area in 1998, following completion of an Environmental Impact Statement undertaken by the Price BLM in response to proposed coalbed natural-gas development in the area. More than 1,100 OG wells were present in the study area in 2006. Active nests on federal lands in the Price study area typically were protected from surface disturbing activities within 0.8 km during the nesting season, although exceptions were occasionally granted based on topography and other considerations. Helicopter surveys conducted once per year during May from 1998–2006 aided in identification of 264 Golden Eagle (*Aquila chrysaetos*), Red-tailed Hawk (*B. jamaicensis*), and Prairie Falcon (*Falco mexicanus*) nest clusters in the study area.

The Rawlins study area consisted of rolling topography interspersed with rocky escarpments. The vegetation was predominantly sagebrush (*Artemisia* spp.)-grassland and desert shrubs. The Rawlins BLM identified 13 Key Raptor Areas within the Rawlins Field Office (FO) and the study area supports one of the largest known breeding populations of Ferruginous Hawks. Rapid expansion of OG development activities began in the study area during the 1980s. As of 2006, there were more than 4,200 OG wells in the study area. As in the Price area, active nests in the Rawlins study area on federal lands were typically protected from surface-disturbing activities within 0.8 km, although exceptions were occasionally granted for similar reasons. Raptor nests were surveyed opportunistically in the area with some degree of regularity beginning in 1978. During the 1980s OG expansion, Ferruginous Hawks began attempting to nest on OG structures and commonly failed. In response to this situation, the BLM erected 105 ANSs between 1987 and 2002, and began intensively monitoring nesting activities on these structures in 1988. Additionally, more intensive surveys (primarily from the ground) of all raptor species nesting in the area began in 1998. Nest surveys conducted between 1978 and 2006 aided in the identification of 1,109 Golden Eagle, Ferruginous Hawk, Red-tailed Hawk, and Prairie Falcon nest clusters in the study area.

We compiled existing data on Golden Eagle, Red-tailed Hawk, and Prairie Falcon nests and OG development activities in the Price study area for 1998–2006. We compiled existing data on Golden Eagles, Ferruginous Hawks, Red-tailed Hawks, and Prairie Falcons and OG development activities in the Rawlins study area for 1978–2006. We grouped individual nests into nest clusters (analogous to the concept of nesting territories maintained by individual pairs, but unrelated to evaluation of territorial defense behaviors) based on spatial relationships and individual nest histories. For analytical purposes, we classified all nest clusters on an annual basis in two ways: "used" (i.e., evidence of nest attendance or actual nesting obtained) versus "unused" or "active" (i.e., egg laying confirmed) versus "other." We classified OG wells as new or established in relation to each survey-year nesting season. We compiled road layers from existing data files and augmented them through digitization of additional roads within a geographic information system (GIS) based on 2006 aerial photographs (1-m resolution). We classified roads as primary, secondary, or OG; additionally, we assigned establishment years for wellhead roads (i.e., road segments dead-ending at a single well) based on the associated well. We merged and reduced available high-resolution vegetation layers for each study area to individual layers containing 22 and 19 vegetation variables for the Price and Rawlins study areas, respectively. We obtained climatic data on pre-nesting-season winter precipitation, the Palmer Drought Severity Index (PDSI), and previous-year PDSI for each study area and relevant survey year. We acknowledge that other factors, such as prey availability, distribution of power lines, and livestock grazing, also may influence nesting raptors, but we were unable to retrospectively characterize these factors to our satisfaction.

From the collected and compiled datasets, we calculated individual nest-cluster development and vegetation metrics for each survey year. We calculated development metrics within 0.8-km and 2.0-km radii of nests, and vegetation metrics at the 2.0-km scale. We reduced suites of vegetation and development variables down to more manageable and orthogonal datasets using principal components analysis (PCA). We associated climate variables with nest clusters by study area and year. We used descriptive statistics, analysis of variance (ANOVA), and GIS software to describe changes in development near nest clusters, and spatial relationships between development and nest clusters. We used model-building techniques, specifically variable selection and Akaike's information criterion (AIC), to assess annual and multi-year relationships between the status of nest clusters and development, vegetation, and climate metrics. We also modeled Ferruginous Hawk nest success and productivity in the Rawlins study area in relation to these variables and nest accessibility. Finally, we assessed the ability of ANSs to alter the response of Ferruginous Hawks to OG development and the species' general nesting ecology and behavior.

Results and Discussion

Price, Utah Study Area

In the Price study area, the number of OG wells increased from 451 to 1,177 between 1998 and 2006. The most dramatic increase in wells near nest clusters occurred from 1999–2002, corresponding to the period of greatest OG development. Over the study period, the distance between nest clusters and the nearest OG well decreased significantly and the number of wells near clusters increased significantly. The percentage of nest clusters with no wells nearby decreased by ~19% at both the 0.8-km (90% to 71%) and 2.0-km (73% to 54%) scales.

We identified three OG-development "hotspots" (i.e., areas with significant increases in well density between 1998 and 2006) in the Price study area and associated, proximate nest clusters with at least 5 years of survey history. Only Golden Eagle nest clusters had sufficient sample sizes ($n = 43$) for analysis. We found no significant difference between the distance from "used" or "unused" nest clusters and development hotspot centers, but visual inspection of the data did suggest a potential temporary shift of used nests away from development during the period of most intensive OG development. We speculate that this shift may have been temporary due to an eventual habituation of Golden Eagles to OG development in the area.

PCA reduced the original Price development dataset to two development factors (DFs); DF1 reflected changes in OG development (i.e., cover and proximity of OG roads and wells), while DF2 reflected changes in non-OG roads (i.e., cover and proximity of non-OG roads). Investigation of relationships between annual nest-cluster status and development patterns alone (called "development-only" models) revealed that Golden Eagle cluster "use" and "activity" related negatively to OG development (DF1), but positively to non-OG roads (DF2). Red-tailed Hawk cluster use and activity related positively to DF1 at the 0.8-km scale but negatively to DF1 at the 2.0-km scale, and cluster use related positively to DF2 within 0.8 km. Prairie Falcon nest-cluster status did not relate significantly to development factors alone.

When vegetation and climate variables were considered in conjunction with development patterns (called "development-plus" models), annual Golden Eagle cluster status in the Price area was still negatively related to OG development, but positively related to non-OG roads. Variable interactions suggested that negative relationships to OG development were enhanced in human landscapes, habitats dominated by rabbitbrush (*Chrysothamnus*

spp.), and riparian forests. In contrast, the relationship to OG development became positive in open habitats featuring black sagebrush (*A. nova*). We speculate that OG structures may provide beneficial perches for Golden Eagles in low-stature black-sagebrush habitats.

Investigation of development-plus models of annual Red-tailed Hawk cluster use and activity in the Price study area revealed positive relationships with OG development at the 0.8-km scale, but negative relationships at the 2.0-km scale. Additionally, a few models suggested a positive relationship between cluster use and non-OG roads within 0.8 km. These are the same relationships revealed by the development-only models; however, variable interactions suggested that positive cluster-activity relationships with development were muted in riparian forest, grass, and forb habitats. We suggest that any "benefits" of development accrued to nesting Red-tailed Hawks in the dominant pinyon-juniper (*Pinus edulis* or *monophylla-Juniperus* spp.) habitats of the Price study area from creation of open hunting areas and/or changes in prey abundance may not carry over to riparian and grass/forb habitats, because the latter habitats likely already contain adequate perches, hunting areas, and prey resources for Red-tailed Hawks.

When we examined development-plus models of annual Prairie Falcon nest-cluster status in the Price study area, we found that cluster use related positively to OG development at both spatial scales when we considered each DF1 scale variable alone, but related negatively to DF1 at the 2.0-km scale when we considered both DF1 variables simultaneously. Additionally, Prairie Falcon cluster use and activity both related negatively to non-OG roads, perhaps reflecting sensitivity to closely intruding recreational roads. Note that the development-only models revealed no significant relationships with development for Prairie Falcons. We also caution that Price-area Prairie Falcons were represented by the smallest sample sizes, and model results therefore should be interpreted with particular caution.

We also attempted to investigate longer-term relationships by assessing proportional cluster use and activity (i.e., the proportion of years surveyed during which a particular cluster was used or active) relative to development and vegetation. Sample sizes limited our ability to assess such relationships to Golden Eagles, and top models of proportional use and activity for this species accounted for only 13–15% of explainable variation in cluster status. Top models suggested that proportional use and activity related positively to the variance in OG development and non-OG road levels. We speculate that the indicated relationships may reflect more consistent use and activity of nest clusters containing greater diversity of either type of development (i.e., higher habitat diversity and therefore more nesting options). We caution, however, that clusters selected for the proportional analyses were more likely to be in development hotspots, given the focus of monitoring efforts in such areas.

Considering the dynamics of all three species in the Price study area revealed mixed relationships with development. Only Golden Eagles exhibited consistent, negative relationships with OG development and at both spatial scales. In contrast, both Red-tailed Hawks and Prairie Falcons apparently benefited from proximate OG development (within 0.8 km), but this relationship reversed or diminished at the broader 2.0-km scale. Golden Eagles and Red-tailed Hawks exhibited some positive relationships with non-OG roads, whereas Prairie Falcons exhibited fairly consistent negative relationships with this factor. Vegetation and climate variables were influential in top models of use and/or activity for all three species. Specifically, the cluster status of all three species related positively to wetter current year conditions, but drier pre-nesting winters.

Rawlins, Wyoming Study Area

In the Rawlins study area, the number of wells increased from 1,438 to 4,258 between 1978 and 2006. The number of wells near nest clusters increased most dramatically from 1978–1985 and 1994–2006, two periods of intensified development. The total length of roads within 2.0 km of nest clusters increased significantly between 1978 and 2006. Additionally (and similar to Price), the distance between nest clusters and OG wells decreased significantly and the number of nearby wells increased significantly across this period. The percentage of nest clusters with no wells nearby declined by 9% at the 0.8-km (95% to 86%) and 12% at the 2.0-km (86% to 74%) scale.

We identified three OG-development hotspots in the Rawlins study area and associated nest clusters with a minimum of 5 years of survey history from 1998–2006. Cluster sample sizes were sufficient for analysis only for Ferruginous Hawks ($n = 54$). Used and active Ferruginous Hawk clusters were closer to development centers than unused or other clusters. This relationship likely was driven by a shift to nesting on OG structures and ANSs beginning in the late 1980s, as supported by a graphical assessment of the densities of active nest clusters pre- and post-ANS installation.
PCA reduced the original Rawlins development dataset

to two development factors, DF1 and DF2, with interpretations comparable to those for the Price study area. Development-only models revealed that the annual nest-cluster status of Golden Eagles and Red-tailed Hawks related negatively to OG development and positively to non-OG roads at both spatial scales. Ferruginous Hawk non-ANS cluster status relationships were similar, but slightly more complex. Use and activity generally related negatively to OG development, but positively to non-OG roads. However, when DF1 or DF2 entered a model from both spatial scales simultaneously, these relationships reversed at the 2.0-km scale. In contrast, Ferruginous Hawk ANS cluster use and activity both increased with OG development measured at either scale, and non-OG roads within 2 km, but decreased with non-OG roads at the smaller scale. Annual Prairie Falcon cluster status related negatively to both OG development and non-OG roads at both scales.

Development-plus models of annual status suggested that development did not influence Golden Eagle nest-cluster use in the Rawlins area. Instead, vegetation appeared to influence both use and activity similarly and both were apparently greater during drought recovery years (i.e., wet years on the heels of dry years). In contrast, development-plus cluster activity models revealed a negative relationship with OG development at the 2.0-km scale.

Top development-plus models of Rawlins area non-ANS Ferruginous Hawks suffered from poor fit. However, in general annual models suggested that cluster use and activity related positively to non-OG roads within 0.8 km, but that this relationship reversed at the larger spatial scale. Top models also suggested that cluster activity related negatively to OG development within 0.8 km. Variable interactions suggested that the positive influence of non-OG roads at the smaller scale was enhanced in areas with greater cover of evergreen forest, but less Wyoming big sagebrush (*A. tridentata wyomingensis*) and agriculture. We speculate that this relationship may have resulted from either roads providing beneficial openings in forested habitats or, perhaps, a spurious effect of survey bias associated with surveying from roads in such habitats.

Top models of Rawlins ANS Ferruginous Hawk cluster status also suffered from poor fit. However, the models suggested that relationships between cluster status and development were the opposite of those identified for non-ANS clusters. That is, ANS cluster use and activity related negatively to non-OG roads within 0.8 km, but this relationship reversed at the larger scale. Additionally, cluster use and activity related positively to OG development at the 0.8-km scale. We suggest that the positive relationship with OG development at ANS clusters may be related to changes in prey abundance and availability associated with OG development in combination with the security provided by these inaccessible nests (and hence a tolerance for development activities). Variable interactions suggested that the positive influence of OG development at the smaller spatial scale was enhanced in areas with more riparian forest, grass, mountain mahogany (*Cercocarpus* spp.), and agriculture. The effect appeared driven by a few ANS clusters with relatively more OG development, grass cover, and high annual use and activity. We speculate that OG-mediated changes to prey abundance and accessibility, access to prime natural habitat (grass), and secure ANS nest sites may have caused the observed interaction.

Top development-plus models of annual Red-tailed Hawk cluster status in the Rawlins study area suggested that cluster use related negatively to OG development at the 0.8-km scale, but positively related to OG development at the 2.0-km scale. This suggests that Red-tailed Hawks may be relatively tolerant of OG activities in the larger landscape, but not in the immediate vicinity of the nest. This pattern is the opposite of the relationships detected for Price-area Red-tailed Hawks. Variable interactions suggested that the positive association with OG development within 2.0 km was enhanced in grass, forested, or agriculture landscapes, but muted in habitats dominated by Wyoming big sagebrush. Additionally, cluster use related negatively to non-OG roads within 2.0 km. In contrast to these cluster use relationships, top models of Red-tailed Hawk cluster activity revealed no relationships with development factors.

Annual development-plus models of Prairie Falcon cluster use and activity suggested negative relationships with both OG development and non-OG roads. The development-plus model results were similar to those produced when we considered development factors alone. Variable interactions suggested that the negative relationships to OG development were enhanced in barren landscapes, but diminished in Wyoming big sagebrush. We speculate that increased prey accessibility associated with OG activities in sagebrush habitats, but no clear benefit in open, barren landscapes, may drive this relationship. Our results appear to suggest that Rawlins-area Prairie Falcons were the most sensitive to both types of development (i.e., OG and non-OG roads), but these results must be interpreted with caution given the smaller sample sizes available for this species.

As in Price, sample sizes limited our comparison of longer-term trends in the Rawlins study area. However, we were able to assess proportional cluster-status relationships for Golden Eagles and non-ANS Ferruginous Hawks. The top models of Golden Eagle proportional cluster status performed well, accounting for 44–54% of the explainable variance. Golden Eagle cluster use and activity models suggested a positive association with areas containing more OG development, but with less change in development (i.e., variance) over time. Additionally, proportional cluster use and activity were positively associated with areas of greater and more variable non-OG road metrics. This suggests that Rawlins Golden Eagles were tolerant of OG activity, as long as development did not occur too rapidly. Additionally, use and activity were apparently greater in clusters with a greater diversity in levels of non-OG roads (perhaps reflecting more diverse foraging or nesting options).

Rawlins area non-ANS Ferruginous Hawk proportional use and activity models revealed a negative relationship with OG development at the 0.8-km scale, but the opposite relationship at the 2.0-km scale. Proportional use and activity also related positively to non-OG roads within 0.8 km, but also the amount of change in non-OG road levels over time. Similar to Rawlins Golden Eagles, this association with greater variance in non-OG roads may reflect an attraction to greater development heterogeneity. As with Golden Eagles, the top Ferruginous Hawk proportional cluster status models performed well, explaining 35–38% of the variance. The general agreement between the poor-fitting annual models and better-performing proportional models bolsters our confidence in the non-ANS Ferruginous Hawk relationships. That is, both analyses suggested that, at the 0.8-km scale, cluster use and activity related negatively to OG development, but positively to non-OG roads.

We attempted to model Rawlins Ferruginous Hawk nest success and productivity at accessible (mostly natural) and inaccessible (mostly manmade, including ANSs) nests, but produced few, mostly poor-fitting models. Nevertheless, the models generally suggested that success and productivity at accessible nests were largely independent of development, while success and productivity at inaccessible nests related positively to OG development, but negatively to non-OG roads. Overall, accessible nests had lower success (63 vs. 94%) and productivity (1.6 vs. 2.7 large [≥80% of fledging age] chicks produced per nesting attempt) than inaccessible nests. We suggest that accessibility was the overriding driver of success and productivity, and therefore, other variables (i.e., development, vegetation, and climate) were of less importance to Ferruginous Hawk reproductive output, resulting in poor model fit.

A comparison of the relationships identified in the Rawlins study area revealed some common trends among species. Overall, cluster use and activity of all four species (excluding ANS Ferruginous Hawks, a special case) in the Rawlins study area related negatively to OG development at both the 0.8 and 2.0-km scales. Additionally, non-ANS Ferruginous Hawks, Red-tailed Hawks, and Prairie Falcons exhibited negative relationships with non-OG roads at the 2.0-km scale. Only the status of non-ANS Ferruginous Hawk clusters related positively to non-OG roads, and this occurred at the smaller spatial scale. Vegetation and climate factors were influential in at least some top models of cluster use and activity for each species. In particular, the proportion of forest, grassland, and agriculture relative to sagebrush in the landscape appeared to be important to cluster status. The nesting activity of all four species also responded positively to a "drought recovery" pattern; i.e., improved during wetter years with more winter precipitation when such conditions followed a drier year.

Overall Conclusions

Both the Price and Rawlins study areas experienced significant OG development during the study periods with apparent effects on raptor breeding activity. We found more consistent evidence of negative impacts of OG development in the Rawlins study area, with all four focal species exhibiting negative impacts at either the 0.8 or 2.0-km scale. Nesting raptors in both study areas also exhibited negative relationships with current-year drought severity. Our results suggest that the inclusion of vegetation and climate variables consistently modified relationships between nesting status and development. Additionally, Rawlins nesting activity appeared to increase in drought recovery years (i.e., wetter years and pre-season winters following drier years). Additional climatic detail and data on prey abundance would likely have improved our ability to model nest-status relationships.

Given the retrospective nature of this study, we stress that our results suggest correlations only; clear cause-effect inferences cannot be assumed. We have made every effort to acknowledge the limitations and weaknesses of the datasets used and results produced, but also point out that better-suited datasets do not currently exist and are unlikely to be forthcoming in the near future. That said, our results suggested that OG development produced negative effects for species with the largest sample sizes in both the Price (i.e., Golden Eagles) and Rawlins (i.e., Golden Eagles and non-ANS Ferruginous Hawks) study areas. Our results suggest that current management stipulations applied in the two study areas (i.e., 0.8-km radius buffers during the nesting season) should not be reduced, as Price-area Golden Eagles and Rawlins-area Ferruginous Hawks, Red-tailed Hawks, and Prairie Falcons exhibited negative relationships with OG development that occurred within 0.8 km of nest clusters. Additionally, current stipulations may be insufficient to avoid negative impacts to nesting raptors, as we also detected negative relationships between OG development and Price-area Golden Eagles and Rawlins-area Golden Eagles and Prairie Falcons at the broader 2.0-km spatial scale. Unfortunately, we were unable to evaluate effectively potential population-level impacts of development due to limitations in the existing raptor datasets.

Acknowledgements

Funding for this research project was provided by the U.S. Department of Energy through the BLM Utah State Office (BLM Assistance Agreement JSA065003).

The initial study plan for this project benefited from reviews provided by members of the Raptor Radii Project BLM Steering Committee, which included Dave Mills (BLM Utah, Richfield Field Office), Steve Madsen (BLM Utah State Office), Dave Roberts (BLM Wyoming State Office), and Wes Anderson (BLM Colorado State Office). Additional semi-independent reviews were provided by members of a more extensive core "working group" that helped to oversee the project and other vested individuals, including Chris Colt (Fishlake National Forest, formerly UDWR Price Field Office), Mark Fuller (U.S. Geological Survey, Idaho), and Ed Hollowed and Brett Smithers (BLM White River Field Office, Colorado). Independent technical reviews by Karen Steenhof (U.S. Geological Survey, Idaho), Tom Thurow (University of Wyoming), and Jim Watson (Washington Department of Fish and Wildlife) further improved the study plan.

This final technical note benefited from initial reviews by members of the BLM Steering Committee, Chris Colt, and Mark Fuller, as well as independent reviews by Fred Adler (Department of Mathematics, University of Utah), Michael Kochert (U.S. Geological Survey, Idaho), Gwyn McKee (Thunderbird-Jones & Stokes, Inc., Wyoming), and Jim Watson (Washington Department of Fish and Wildlife).

Oil and Gas Development and Raptors

Currently ~15 million ha of western lands managed by the Bureau of Land Management (BLM) are leased for gas, oil, or geothermal energy production (BLM 2005). Although recent large-scale expansions in domestic oil and gas (OG) extraction activities are likely to continue in the United States (see the Energy Policy Act of 2005), very few studies have attempted to investigate the potential implications for nesting raptors (e.g., Harmata 1991, Squires et al. 1993). OG development may affect raptors through direct habitat loss or *disturbance* (we have italicized key terms on first usage to draw the reader's attention to definitions provided in the glossary; please note that scientific names also are italicized per usual practice). While the footprint of individual OG wells is minimal relative to other energy developments (e.g., mining), the total habitat lost to the network of wells and connecting roads can be considerable in areas undergoing full-field development (Postovit and Postovit 1989). The potential for OG-related disturbance of nesting, foraging or roosting raptors arises not only from new well installation activities, including road and pad construction, drilling, and equipment installation over the course of several weeks to months, but also from continual servicing and maintenance of wells over their productive lifetime. Additional potential for disturbance arises from increased public access to areas under OG development (Postovit and Postovit 1989).

Past studies of direct relevance have focused primarily on the relationship between nesting raptors and OG development. Ritchie (1991) reported unusual Gyrfalcon (*Falco rusticolus*) and Rough-legged Hawk (*Buteo lagopus*) nest placements on or near development infrastructure in Alaska (e.g., pipelines or roads). In regards to actual nest productivity, studies focusing on Ferruginous Hawks (*B. regalis*) have reported both no clear effect (Van Horn 1993, Zelenak and Rotella 1997) and higher nest productivity further from development (Harmata 1991). Squires et al. (1993) found a positive correlation between foraging Prairie Falcons (*F. mexicanus*) and density of oil wells in northeastern Wyoming. Note, however, that distance from aeries and amount of grassland habitat were the best predictors of foraging areas, and that wells were coincidentally concentrated in grasslands near the aeries. This example reveals the need for awareness of potential confounding correlations that may exist between development and other habitat characteristics when attempting to understand relationships between raptors and development. Most recently, a study in northeastern Utah on BLM lands revealed that nests of breeding Ferruginous Hawks were associated with high numbers of active (i.e., currently operational) OG wells; however, greater reproductive success was associated with larger distances to the closest active well. Thus, although development of OG wells did not appear to have a negative influence on the suitability of breeding habitat, it appeared that development had a negative influence on reproductive success if active wells occurred too close to nest sites (Keough 2006).

Other raptor "disturbance" studies also may shed light on potential effects of OG development. For example, development activities associated with dam construction (i.e., road construction, vehicle traffic, heavy equipment operation, and blasting) did not appear to influence negatively the behavior or productivity of Prairie Falcons in the Snake River Birds of Prey National Conservation Area (Holthuijzen 1989). In this situation, the position of aeries at least 50 m above development activities may have served to buffer nests from disturbance. The response of raptors to roads can vary by species and traffic volume (Bautista et al. 2004). Unfortunately, studies investigating the more general relationship between raptors and human-altered (primarily by roads and habitations) landscapes have commonly failed to separate the potential influence of disturbance from those of habitat or other environmental changes (e.g., Craighead and Mindell 1981, Bechard et al. 1990, Bosakowski et al. 1993, Berry et al. 1998).

Regardless, several studies have clearly demonstrated the potential disturbance effects of human activities on nesting raptors. White and Thurow (1985) experimentally demonstrated negative effects of human disturbance (i.e., walk-in and drive-up approaches and operation of a motor near nests) on nesting Ferruginous Hawks. A variety of recreational activities also may influence raptors. For example, hikers and pedestrian foot traffic can change the behavior of both nesting (Swenson 1979, Swarthout and Steidl 2003, Watson 2004) and wintering raptors (Fletcher et al. 1999). Similarly, camping activities altered the behavior of nesting Bald Eagles (*Haliaeetus leucocephalus*; Steidl and Anthony 2000) and reproductive output of Ospreys (*Pandion haliaetus*; Swenson 1979). Rock climbing also can be deleterious to cliff-nesting raptors, such as the Peregrine Falcon (*F. peregrinus*; Brambilla et al. 2004). The effects of human disturbance on nesting raptors may be influenced by a number of factors, including proximity, disturbance type, nest exposure, and resource availability (Suter and Joness 1981, White and Thurow 1985, Grubb and King 1991, Grubb et al. 1992). Studies of breeding Bald Eagles suggest that proximity is the most influential characteristic of disturbance, with both horizontal (Grubb and King 1991, Grubb et al. 1992) and vertical (Watson 2004) distance identified as important. A study of Ferruginous Hawk nests in North Dakota illustrated the potential importance of exposure; relatively exposed ground nests were located farther from human development than tree nests (Lokemoen and Duebbert 1976). Disturbance sensitivity also may be greater in years of reduced prey availability (White and Thurow 1985).

In addition to disturbance characteristics, habituation also appears to play a significant role in determining disturbance responses. Observations of raptors exposed to repeated weapons testing or aircraft flyovers suggest raptors may habituate rapidly to disturbances (Andersen et al. 1986, 1989; Brown et al. 1999). For example, Andersen et al. (1989) found that low-level helicopter approaches at Red-tailed Hawk (*B. jamaicensis*) nests in areas with and without previous helicopter activity resulted in flushing of adults at 8% and 53% of nests, respectively. Similarly, Ferruginous Hawks apparently habituated to disturbances present when the adults first arrived on the breeding grounds (White and Thurow 1985).

Recognizing that OG development activities can result in disturbance of nesting raptors has important implications for federal land managers. The Migratory Bird Treaty Act (MBTA) and Bald and Golden Eagle Protection Act (BGEPA) require federal land management agencies to prevent the "take" of raptors, their young, and nests. Additionally, the BGEPA prohibits the disturbance of nesting eagles. In order to comply with MBTA and BGEPA regulations, federal land managers commonly employ spatial and/or temporal nest protections to minimize the potential negative effects of human activities on nesting raptors.

Recommended spatial buffers may vary depending on the species of concern or be comparatively standardized across species. For example, Richardson and Miller (1997) suggest buffers of 200–1,600 m for Golden Eagles (*Aquila chrysaetos*), 200–800 km for Ferruginous Hawks, and 50–800 m for Prairie Falcons. In contrast, Romin and Muck (2002) recommend buffers of 0.8 km (0.5 mile) for Golden Eagles and Ferruginous Hawks, and 0.4 km (0.25 mile) buffers for Prairie Falcons. Suter and Joness (1981) have suggested that these three

species are the most disturbance-sensitive raptors likely to encounter energy development in the West. Previous recommendations concerning temporal buffers suggest that nesting areas should be protected from the time of adult arrival through at least the first few weeks after hatch (Suter and Joness 1981, Romin and Muck 2002). Evidence suggests that nesting raptors may be less sensitive to disturbance after hatching (White and Thurow 1985).

Currently, raptor nest-protection standards vary considerably across the interior West and generally are based on limited information about the actual effects of different types of potential disturbances on specific raptor species. One recent attempt to develop and promote standardized spatial and temporal disturbance-buffer guidelines was compiled by the Utah Field Office of the U.S. Fish and Wildlife Service (Romin and Muck 2002, first edition produced in 1999). These guidelines were based on a thorough review of published information on disturbance responses and thresholds from a variety of previous studies. The recommendations contained therein generally are applied now throughout Utah, and have received some attention by federal and state agencies in surrounding states. However, although these guidelines were based on the best available disturbance-related data, it is clear that a number of species and relevant disturbance types (e.g., OG development) are underrepresented. The general lack of data in support of specific raptor protection guidelines for use on BLM-managed lands (e.g., through implementation of Best Management Practices) was partially responsible for the establishment of this research project.

The Raptor Radii Research Project

In June 2006, HawkWatch International (HWI) was selected by the BLM to serve as the Principal Investigator (BLM Assistance Agreement JSA065003) of what was intended to be a three-year research project initially funded by the U.S. Department of Energy through the BLM (Intragovernmental Order DE-A126-06NT15467) to investigate the potential disturbance effects of OG development activities on nesting raptors in Utah, Wyoming, and Colorado. This "Raptor Radii Research Project" was originally envisioned to encompass two phases. The objective of Phase I was to compile and evaluate historical data relevant to relationships between natural-gas extraction activities and the distribution, abundance, and nest-site occupancy of raptors in the BLM Price Field Office (FO) in southeastern Utah (focus on coalbed natural gas [CBNG] extraction) and the BLM Rawlins FO in south-central Wyoming (focus on conventional natural-gas extraction). Phase II was envisioned to comprise a 1–2 year field experiment across study areas in Utah, Wyoming, and Colorado to quantify the distances and seasonal times at which OG development activities have undesirable effects on nesting raptors; however, for various complicated reasons, Phase II did not proceed as planned. The ultimate goal of this research was to provide guidance for applying protective spatial and temporal buffers to minimize unwanted disturbance to nesting raptors exposed to OG activities. This document presents the results of our Phase I investigations.

Goals and Objectives

Phase I of the Raptor Radii Project was designed to assemble and use historical data available from the BLM Price and Rawlins FOs in Wyoming and Utah, respectively, to learn about relationships between various aspects of the development and operation of oil and natural-gas extraction activities and the abundance, distribution, nest-site occupancy, and, where possible, nesting success and productivity of selected raptor species. Because this effort relied solely on historical datasets, another major goal of the project was to identify the limitations of existing datasets and past survey strategies and provide recommendations for their improvement.

The specific goals of this Phase I research were to:

Goal 1. Compile existing historical data to evaluate their usefulness for quantifying and describing the relationship between coincident natural-gas field development, production, and maintenance operations and raptor nesting activities.

Goal 2. Where suited to the task, use available raptor monitoring data and documentation of the type, time, and extent of development activities to evaluate the effectiveness of raptor spatial and temporal buffer restrictions that have been applied on the study sites.

Goal 3. Based on these assessments, evaluate whether these historical datasets were useful for quantifying the relationship between OG development activities and nesting raptors, including identifying those data that were not useful for this purpose, explaining why they were not useful, recommending necessary improvements or standards that would provide stronger inference, and developing objectives for use of these data in guiding future development.

We address the first two goals outlined above in this document and address the third goal in a separate document (Smith et al. 2010). In regards to the first two goals, an investigation into the relevant data available from each study area (outlined below) and the inherent limits associated with these datasets guided our formulation of specific research objectives, which were as follows:

Objective 1. Describe temporal trends in development near focal-species nest clusters in the Price and Rawlins study areas.

Objective 2. Described distributional patterns of nest-cluster status in relation to development in the Price and Rawlins study areas.

Objective 3. Assess relationships between nest-cluster status and development in the Price and Rawlins study areas.

Objective 4. Assess Ferruginous Hawk nest success and productivity in the Rawlins study area.

Objective 5. Assess the response of Ferruginous Hawks to *artificial nest structures* (ANSs) in the Rawlins study area.

Nest Cluster Focus

It is critical for the reader to understand that throughout the majority of this report we focus on *nest clusters*, rather than individual nests, as the unit of research interest. Among most raptor species, individual breeding pairs often maintain variable numbers of clustered, alternative nest sites (Steenhof and Newton 2007). Although more than one nest may be maintained (i.e., tended) in a particular year by a breeding pair, actual nesting and laying of eggs will occur in only one nest. This suggests that the appropriate sample unit for multi-year assessments of raptor nesting activity is what we term the nest cluster (analogous to the "nesting territory" definition used by Steenhof and Newton [2007] but avoids potential confusion related to the ethologists' concept of territoriality). The nest-cluster approach reduces alternate nests associated with individual breeding pairs to a single sample unit and avoids issues of pattern dilution that may arise from the retention of every individual nest. We outline below the procedures we used to identify species-specific nest clusters.

Study Areas and Background Information

The two study areas included in this project were selected based on extensive multi-year raptor nest monitoring that occurred in each area coincident with extensive OG development.

Price, Utah Study Area

The Price study area was delineated based on the extent of nesting data collected by the Utah Division of Wildlife Resources (UDWR) and past OG development activities on lands primarily managed by the BLM Price FO in southeastern Utah (Figure 1). The study area is approximately 21,200 km² (including both public and private lands) in size and ranges from 1,193–3,521 m in elevation. Canyons and cliffs are common in the study area and pinyon-juniper (*Pinus edulis-Juniperus* spp.) woodlands predominate, interspersed with sagebrush (*Artemisia* spp.) and grass openings. The area received an annual average of 24 cm of precipitation from 1998–2006 (NOAA 2007).

The first relatively comprehensive raptor inventory was conducted in the area in the mid-1990s when heightened

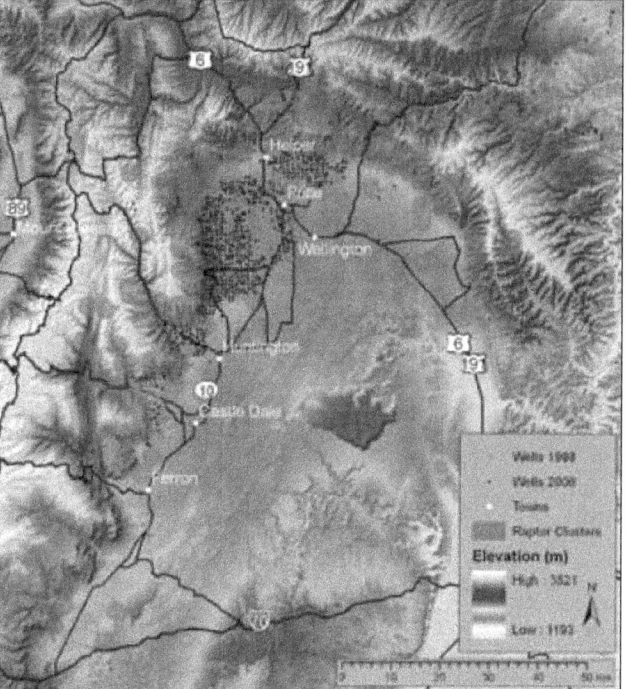

Figure 1. Map showing the locations of active oil and gas wells in 1998 and 2006 in relation to 264 raptor nest clusters in the Price, Utah study area. Raptor clusters are represented by 2-km buffers extending around the individual Golden Eagle, Red-tailed Hawk, and Prairie Falcon nests included in each cluster; we included only clusters used at least once during the 1998–2006 raptor survey period to create the buffers shown.

interest in developing the natural-gas resources of the area began to emerge (Bates and Moretti 1994, Parrish 1995). Raptor data were collected only opportunistically prior to this period. Following completion of an area-wide Environmental Impact Statement (EIS) in 1997 related to proposed expansion of CBNG activities in the area west of Price, UDWR began implementing annual helicopter surveys in 1998 focused on documenting the nesting activities of primary nesting raptors in the area (BLM 1997). This survey was a requirement of the EIS, for which Conoco-Phillips, the primary industry corporation now involved in developing the natural-gas resources in the area, has been the primary financier.

As of 2006, there were more than 1,100 wells in the Price study area, with a nearly uniform distribution of well pads at a density of one per quarter section (160-acre spacing). In a few cases, the uniformity of well-pad distribution was modified intentionally from the start to accommodate topographic constraints and maintain an EIS-mandated 0.8 km (0.5 mile) nesting season (1 February – 15 July) buffer around nest sites on federal lands occupied during the previous three years (BLM 1997). In some cases, the BLM granted industry-requested variances to allow development of new well pads within 0.8 km of known nest sites when landscape screening visually separated well pads from nest sites. In other cases, development occurred unintentionally in closer proximity to existing nest sites because the nest sites were not discovered until after the development had proceeded. In addition, a number of land sections within the Conoco-Phillips domain are administered by the State of Utah, wherein development generally has proceeded with few constraints. These areas therefore provide other cases where wells have been installed in closer proximity to nests and sometimes within the nesting season.

Since 1998, UDWR and Conoco-Phillips personnel have conducted helicopter surveys in the study area once per year during May (survey dates 8–30 May 1998–2006). They selected this survey period to allow for determination of nest activity while minimizing potential early-season disturbance to nesting Golden Eagles, the most abundant nesting raptor in the area, and other common area nesters, such as Red-tailed Hawks and Prairie Falcons. The available data included records for 860 nests of these three species distributed across the core study area (i.e., in and around the primary development area within the Price FO). Many of the associated nests had only limited survey histories, however, due to their recent addition to the survey effort in areas of recent expansion of energy development. Other nests received only one-time or infrequent surveys in relation to energy speculation, seismic work, exploratory drilling, and mining operations. While nests were monitored much more consistently within the Price CBNG EIS area, a number of nests were still missed each year, partly due to the difficulty and high cost of helicopter surveys. Of 264 identifiable nest clusters with at least one year of confirmed nesting activity identified across the core study area for the three focal species, 129 Golden Eagle, 23 Red-tailed Hawk, and 9 Prairie Falcon nest clusters had at least five years of survey history between 1998 and 2006.

The primary information available for nests in this survey area was the presence/absence of breeding pairs that had succeeded to the late-incubation or early brood-rearing stage. Although limited brood-size data were collected opportunistically, reliable annual productivity estimates were not possible because of the timing and limited number (once annually) of surveys and the variable stages of surveyed nests.

Rawlins, Wyoming Study Area

The Rawlins study area was selected based on the extent of nesting data collected by the BLM Rawlins FO and associated nearby OG development activities that occurred predominantly on lands managed by this FO in south-central Wyoming (Figure 2). The study area is approximately 44,400 km^2 (including both public and private lands) in size and ranges from 1,502–3,663 m in elevation. Rolling hills interspersed with rocky escarpments are common topographic features, while sagebrush-grasslands and other desert shrubs dominate the vegetation. Annual average precipitation was 29 cm from 1978–2006 (NOAA 2007). Thirteen Key Raptor Areas have been identified within the Rawlins FO, and the area contains important nesting habitat for a variety raptors.

In particular, the Rawlins FO encompasses important habitat for the Ferruginous Hawk; south-central Wyoming supports one of the largest known breeding populations of this species (Olendorff 1993). The species is currently listed as a state sensitive species in Wyoming and in most other states where it occurs, and garners similar recognition in several state-level and bird conservation region plans developed by the overarching Partners in Flight avian conservation program (Rich et al. 2004). Rapid expansion of OG development activities in the Rawlins FO in the 1980s stimulated interest among BLM biologists in monitoring and assessing the potential impacts of such development on the Ferruginous Hawks nesting in the area. Several industry companies have been involved in natural-gas development in the Rawlins FO; primary players include BP-Amoco, Williams, Forest Oil, and Anadarko Petroleum Corporation. Wyoming began to experience a boom in OG exploration and development in the late 1970s. By 2006, more than 4,200 OG wells were in the study area. Compared to the Price study area, wells are much less regularly distributed throughout the Rawlins study area, reaching high densities of one well per quarter section (160-acre spacing) in some areas, but with lower densities in others. However, much of the past development activity was concentrated in the open sagebrush and grassland dominated landscapes commonly used as nesting habitat by the Ferruginous Hawk, as well as species such as the Golden Eagle and Prairie Falcon. Similar to the Price study area, Rawlins area nests on federal lands were generally protected by a 0.8-km nesting season (1 February – 31 July) buffer, although exceptions were occasionally granted after consideration of topographic screening or other factors (BLM 1990).

Initial raptor nest monitoring in the FO was sporadic and largely opportunistic, but at least some minimal

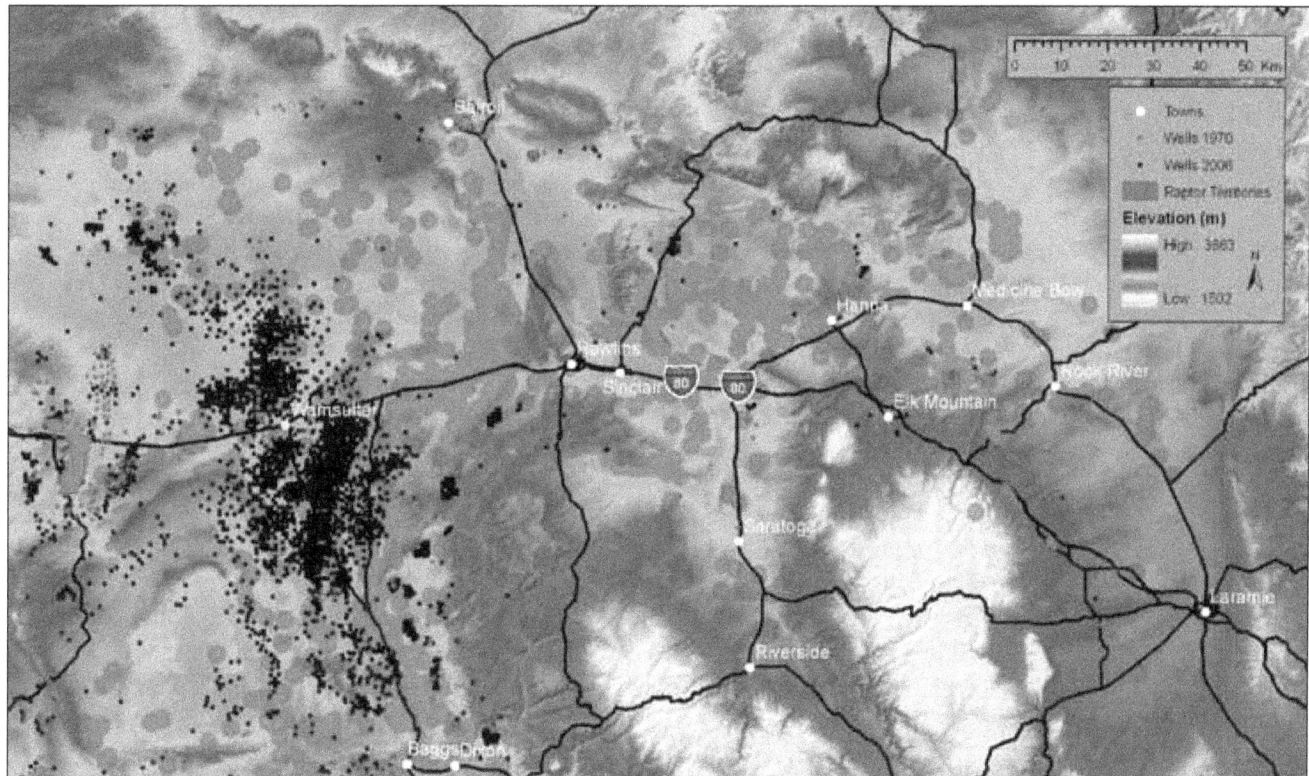

Figure 2. Map showing the locations of active oil and gas wells in 1970 and 2006 in relation to 1,109 raptor nest clusters in the Rawlins, Wyoming study area. Raptor clusters are represented by 2-km buffers extending around the individual Golden Eagle, Ferruginous Hawk, Red-tailed Hawk, and Prairie Falcon nests included in each cluster; only clusters used at least once during the 1970-2006 raptor survey period were used to create the buffers shown.

monitoring effort was made each year beginning in 1978. However, as natural-gas development expanded in the Rawlins FO, Ferruginous Hawks quickly began attempting to exploit natural-gas structures (primarily condensation tanks) as nesting substrates. Equally quickly, it became apparent that this was a recipe for disaster, as such nests regularly failed due to human disturbance related to maintenance of the structures (Tigner and Call 1996). Accordingly, in an attempt to improve nesting habitat for the species and offset the effects of natural-gas development, between 1987 and 2002 the BLM and certain natural-gas companies cooperated in erecting 100 ANSs for Ferruginous Hawks and five other ANSs in the FO. The Ferruginous Hawk ANSs extended 2.5-m above the ground and supported a 1-m² nest platform (see Tigner and Call [1996] for an illustration). ANSs were installed near (i.e., within 1 km) natural-gas extraction facilities to provide alternative substrates for birds that otherwise attempted to nest on associated structures, but also in areas away from development activities to provide alternatives for birds that previously nested on collapsed or otherwise poor-quality natural nests.

Coincident with this effort, in 1988 the BLM initiated a program to monitor nesting activities associated

with all of the installed ANSs. Largely opportunistic monitoring of various natural nests and other species continued to occur through 1997 in conjunction with the ANS monitoring. Then in 1998, the BLM initiated a more intensive, initially largely volunteer driven effort to expand their annual monitoring to cover most known Ferruginous Hawk nests in the FO with a recent history of use (i.e., within the past 5–10 years), as well as attempt to collect at least presence–absence data for other raptor species nesting in the area. Each year nest searches included some areas not known to have been used previously by Ferruginous Hawks, but no standardized sampling design was applied. After 1999, paid seasonal technicians conducted the survey effort. At this time, Mike Neal (now an HWI employee) took over as the BLM seasonal field supervisor of this effort, a capacity in which he continued to serve annually through 2004. He also developed his Master's thesis based on this project (Neal 2007).

The surveys conducted beginning in 1998 focused on assessing the *breeding status* (i.e., *breeding* or *non-breeding*), *nesting success* (i.e., *successful* or *failed*), and *productivity* (i.e., number of nestlings produced to at least 80% of fledging age) of all ANS and many natural Ferruginous Hawk nests in the study area with a documented history of use. Monitoring data for other species also were collected opportunistically during this period, as before. All surveys were conducted on the ground. Surveys to document initial nesting activity were conducted during April and May, with follow-up surveys in June and July to document nesting success and productivity. A total of 3,475 individual nest locations of Ferruginous Hawks, Golden Eagles, Red-tailed Hawks, and Prairie Falcons were recorded effectively in the BLM dataset we were given to work with. These nests comprised 1,109 identifiably distinct, species-specific nest clusters for which at least one year of nesting activity was confirmed. Of these, 317 Ferruginous Hawk clusters, 116 Golden Eagle clusters, 44 Red-tailed Hawk clusters, and 33 Prairie Falcon clusters had at least 5 years of survey history since the late 1970s. When constrained to the period 1998–2006 (period of best survey coverage), however, these numbers dropped to 240 Ferruginous Hawk, 50 Golden Eagle, 18 Red-tailed Hawk, and 9 Prairie Falcon clusters. The information of value for the latter three species was largely limited to breeding status, as success and productivity were collected much too inconsistently for species other than the Ferruginous Hawk.

Description of Datasets and Data Preparation

We gathered historical datasets of nests monitored in the Price and Rawlins FOs, available OG well information, and other relevant Geographic Information System (GIS) datasets and information available for each study area.

Raptor Nest Data

a. Nest-site coordinates for Golden Eagles, Red-tailed Hawks, and Prairie Falcons monitored in the Price FO from 1998–2006 provided by the UDWR.

b. Nest-site coordinates for Golden Eagles, Ferruginous Hawks, Red-tailed Hawks, and Prairie Falcons monitored in the Rawlins FO from 1970–2006 provided by the BLM.

c. Activity status (i.e., breeding, *tended* or non-breeding) for surveyed nests in both study areas, though often intermittent for individual nests from year to year.

d. Nesting success and productivity data for a subset of Ferruginous Hawk nests in the Rawlins FO. Limited nestling production data for Golden Eagle nests, but accurate nestling ages rarely determined.

e. All Price FO nests were characterized by substrate type, with the vast majority of surveyed nests located on cliffs.

f. All Rawlins FO nests were characterized by substrate type and height above ground level. All Ferruginous Hawk nests with a history of success also were classified as either accessible or inaccessible to humans (unaided by equipment) and mammalian predators (Neal 2007).

We omitted nests for which no breeding event had been recorded during the monitoring period of interest to remove the influence of nests with incongruent histories. We also omitted some Golden Eagle nest records from the Rawlins study area that lacked adequate information for nest activity status and survey dates.

For both datasets, we classified all nests with known species associations into distinct nest clusters, and then identified subsets of clusters with adequate survey histories for inclusion in longer-term analyses. We identified nest clusters using a combination of GIS nearest-neighbor analysis, consideration of topographic features, and inspection of individual nest histories. We used GIS to identify potential clusters of nests with inter-nest distances less than likely maximum spacing of alternate nests associated with distinct breeding pairs. Due to a scarcity of information on spacing of alternate nests, we selected 3 km to serve as a conservative cut-off search distance, although there is evidence that Golden Eagles may maintain more widely spaced alternates (McGahan 1968). After we identified potential nest-clusters using GIS-based nearest-neighbor analyses, we further refined the cluster classifications by examining spatial relationships of nests relative to distinct topographic features such as ridgelines. That is, an intervening ridgeline may allow for closer-than-usual spacing of nest clusters if they lie on opposite sides of the ridgeline and their placement affords access to independent foraging domains extending away from each side of the ridgeline. Finally, further modification of cluster classifications occurred following inspection of individual nest histories to ensure that all defined clusters contained only nests with non-overlapping use histories. That is, in a given year, breeding by the focal species will have been confirmed in only one nest within each cluster, the only possible exception being uncommon cases where conclusive evidence indicated that the same breeding pair renested in a second nest within their cluster following an early failure.

Oil and Gas Well Data

a. Well surface location coordinates and dates of well spudding (i.e., initiation of drilling) and abandonment (where relevant) from the Utah Division of Oil, Gas and Mining (UDOGM) for 1,245 wells that were active in the Price study area after 1997 and were spudded before 14 June 2006.

b. Well surface location coordinates and dates of well spudding and abandonment (where relevant) from the Wyoming Oil and Gas Conservation Commission (WOGCC) for 6,011 wells that were active in the Rawlins study area after 1969 and spudded before 14 June 2006.

The Price FO well layer required additional work to add drilling dates for ~400 wells drilled prior to 2000, for which no integrated electronic data were currently available. A similar number of wells in the Rawlins FO well layer also were missing temporal attributes. All such data were obtainable, however, by retrieving individual well records accessible from the UDOGM and WOGCC websites.

For each corresponding year of nest-monitoring data, we classified wells as either new (i.e., drilled after 1 June of the previous nesting season in the Price study area [no surveys were conducted after May] or after 1 July in Rawlins study area [to reflect the longer survey window in this area]), established (drilled during or prior to the previous nesting season), or abandoned (ceased operation prior to 15 February of the current nesting year). We omitted from consideration any wells that became non-operational prior to the study period of interest. Our initial goal was to further classify new wells as pre-season (drilled since the previous nesting season, but prior to the nesting season of interest) or in-season (drilled during the nesting season of interest); however, preliminary data inspections suggested that for both study areas the number of raptor nests within even 2 km, let alone 0.8 km (typical 0.5-mile buffer), of in-season wells was insufficient to support robust analyses.

Road Data

We obtained GIS data layers of road networks in each study area from various sources, but then substantially augmented those layers through digitizing of 1-m-resolution aerial photographs (U.S. Department of Agriculture National Agriculture Imagery Program) taken in 2006. All digitizing occurred at a scale of 1:30,000, focused primarily on augmenting roads related to OG activities (i.e., we created a road to each well location

active during the study period), but also added other easily visible (primary) roads. We added 1,063 km of roads to the Price FO layer, representing 1,527 individual road segments and increasing the total length of roads by 5.3%. For the Rawlins FO, we added 2,910 km of roads, representing 4,352 individual road segments and increasing the total length of roads by 6.6%. The pre-existing road layers classified roads to type, but classifications were not consistent in the two study areas. To suit our particular needs, we classified roads based on the following conventions:

> Primary: major paved roads and other well maintained connecting state or county roads.
>
> Secondary: lesser maintained roads, town roads, unimproved dirt and gravel roads, etc.
>
> Oil & Gas: wellhead roads (roads dead-ending at a single well or well pad), connecting OG roads (roads connecting ≥2 proximate wellhead roads), and haul roads (roads servicing larger fields of development).

Because individual wellhead roads serviced only a single well, we assumed wellhead roads were created during the year of well establishment (i.e., we assigned to these roads establishment years that were used to add wellhead roads to the road layer on an annual basis).

Landcover/Vegetation Data

Price FO, Utah.—We obtained custom vegetation/ landcover layers prepared by the UDWR for the East Manti, South Manti, and West Tavaputs areas (delineated at 1:10,000 scale, using 2002 or newer aerial photographs) and by the U.S. Forest Service for the Manti-La Sal National Forest (1997 version, delineated at 1:16,000 scale). We then merged the two datasets into a 30-m-resolution raster layer and incorporated supplemental information derived from the Southwest ReGAP raster INFO file (USGS National Gap Analysis Program 2004). We reduced and matched landcover categories from the two original layers, initially producing 31 landcover types, which we further collapsed based on high correlations and reduction of rare classes (i.e., combined aspen (*Populus tremuloides*) and aspen/ conifer; alpine and other forbs; spruce-fir (*Picea* spp.-*Abies* spp.), ponderosa pine (*Pinus ponderosa*), and limber pine (*P. flexilis*)/bristlecone pine (*P. aristata*); desert and high desert shrub; grass and desert grass; mountain shrub and mountain mahogany (*Cercocarpus* spp.); wetland and riparian shrub; and deleted silver sagebrush (*A. cana*). The final Price vegetation dataset contained the following 22 variables: grass, forb, sagebrush general, Wyoming big sagebrush (*A. tridentata wyomingensis*), mountain big sagebrush (*A. t. vaseyana*), basin big sagebrush (*A. t. tridentata*), black sagebrush (*A. nova*), rabbitbrush (*Chrysothamnus* spp.), desert shrub, riparian shrub, riparian forest, mountain shrub, oak-maple (*Quercus* spp.-*Acer* spp.), aspen mix, conifer, pinyon-juniper, pinyon, juniper, barren, water, agriculture, and human habitation.

Rawlins FO, Wyoming.—We obtained custom 30-m resolution vegetation/landcover layers prepared at the Wyoming Geographic Information Science Center at the University of Wyoming (Driese and Nibbelink 2005, Rodemaker and Driese 2006). We reclassified landcover categories from two separate maps to match categories in the less detailed of the two, and merged those into a single vegetation layer with 26 initial categories that covered the entire area of interest. We further collapsed these categories based on high correlations between categories and reduction of rare classes (i.e., we combined evergreen, evergreen/deciduous, and evergreen/mixed; dryland and irrigated agriculture; riparian and upland grassland; mountain big sagebrush and mountain big sagebrush/bitterbrush (*Purshia tridentata*); greasewood (*Sarcobatus vermiculatus*) and desert shrub; and Wyoming big sagebrush and Wyoming big sagebrush/black sagebrush). The final Rawlins vegetation dataset contained the following 19 variables: grass, sagebrush/grass, Wyoming big sagebrush, mountain big sagebrush, Wyoming/mountain big sagebrush, basin big sagebrush, desert shrub, mountain mahogany, mesic shrub, riparian shrub, riparian forest, deciduous forest, evergreen forest mix, juniper, barren, disturbed land, water, agriculture, and human habitation.

Climate Data

We obtained monthly precipitation, temperature, and Palmer Drought Severity Index (PDSI) data for state climate divisions encompassing the Wyoming and Price FO regions from the National Climatic Data Center (NOAA 2007). We used data for Climate Division 7 (Southeast) in Utah and for Wyoming Divisions 3 (Green and Bear [River] Drainages) and 10 (Upper Platte [River Drainage]). We then used the monthly data to calculate average temperatures and total precipitation for each pre-nesting-season winter (November–February), and total precipitation and average temperatures and PDSIs for each division and year of interest. After initial evaluation of these data, we determined that average winter temperatures simply did not vary enough on an annual basis to represent a useful index of interannual climatic variation. Not surprisingly, we also found that annual total precipitation and average PDSI values were

highly correlated (Pearson $r = 0.84$ for Price data from 1998–2006; 0.75 for Rawlins data from 1978–2006) and therefore could not be included together in the same analytical models; accordingly, we opted to focus on the more informative PDSI as the variable of interest. Our climatic variables of interest became winter precipitation (WINT_ppt), PDSI, and PDSI of the previous year (PDSI_lyr). We entered these variables into our multivariate models to account for the potential influence of climatic conditions on annual variation in raptor nesting activity and productivity. For example, Steenhof et al. (1997) found that the percentage of Golden Eagle pairs that laid eggs in a given year was influenced negatively by the severity of the preceding winter during periods of low prey abundance.

Other Data

Prey availability can strongly influence raptor nesting activity (e.g., jackrabbit [*Lepus* spp.] abundance for desert-nesting Golden Eagles; Smith and Murphy 1979, Steenhof et al. 1997). In the context of a study such as this, ideally data on prey population abundances and trends should be modeled along with other environmental factors to account for annual and spatial variability in ecosystem and raptor productivity that is unrelated to potential OG development effects. Unfortunately, no useful information on prey populations was available for the two study areas. Hence, our investigations were constrained to using landcover/vegetation and climatic variables as surrogate indicators of ecosystem variability and condition. We acknowledge the potential critical importance of prey availability to nesting raptors and our limited ability to portray it accurately in a retrospective manner due to the absence of reliable prey-monitoring information.

Power-line structures may attract nesting and perching raptors in relatively treeless areas (APLIC 2006). Consequently, the presence of power lines may influence raptor distribution in the relatively short-stature vegetation dominant in the two study areas. Unfortunately, the power-line layers that are currently readily available for the study areas primarily depict high voltage, long-distance transmission lines and do not accurately portray the distribution of shorter-length lines found in both study areas. Power lines and poles also are not easily detectable on currently available aerial photographs.

One other facet of human-related disturbance that may have a distinct impact on habitat quality for nesting raptors in both study areas is livestock grazing. Livestock grazing is purported to have the potential to increase shrub densities and decrease the availability of herbaceous vegetation (Blaisdell et al. 1982, Miller et al. 1994). Such changes can alter raptor prey abundances and vulnerability (see review in Kochert 1999). Again, however, available stocking and grazing activity information for the two study areas was inadequate to account for the potential influence of grazing at the appropriate spatial and temporal scales.

Calculation of GIS-based Metrics

We used ArcGIS 9.2 Spatial Analyst to generate metrics to help describe relationships between raptor nest clusters, OG activities, and the vegetation characteristics surrounding each nest cluster:

1) For each nest cluster, we calculated the distance to the nearest well and road on an annual basis (i.e., the nearest well or road may change across years). For a given year, we designated the currently *active* nest (confirmed breeding attempt) or cluster centroid (when a cluster was inactive or occupied but no breeding attempt was confirmed) as the point of reference for distance calculations. We adopted this protocol for all cluster-based spatial calculations (see below).

2) For each nest cluster, we calculated well and road densities (i.e., total linear length of roads) within 0.8-km (based on the heretofore standard recommended spatial buffer) and 2-km (selected to represent larger landscape characteristics and capture the majority of the home range of the study species) radii on an annual basis.

3) To capture general patterns of vegetation variation near relevant raptor nest clusters, we calculated the coverage of individual vegetation classes within a 2-km radius (i.e., within larger landscape and probable core foraging areas) of all relevant nest-cluster centroids. A centroid-based approach allowed us to initially characterize the vegetation near each nest cluster from a single reference point (i.e., without considering the potentially shifting location of active/occupied nests within a cluster on an annual basis). Additionally, we also used individual nest-cluster survey histories to calculate year-specific coverage of the original vegetation variables (i.e., we used the active nest as the point of reference during years of nest-cluster activity but the cluster centroid during all other years).

Analytical Methods

Below we outline the primary analytical methods we used to address the five research objectives outlined above. Prior to undertaking formal data analyses, we inspected variable distributions to identify potential outliers and determine the need for data transformations. We removed two nest clusters in the Bairoil area of the Rawlins study area due to extremely high well densities (e.g., during their peak OG development years, these clusters were within 2 km of 164 and 262 wells; the next highest well count within 2 km of a nest cluster was 31). We used the square-root transformation to improve the distribution of the distance-to-well and road and total-length-of-road metrics. We applied an arc-sine transformation to all individual vegetation coverage variables before performing the analyses outlined in the previous section

Objective 1: Describe temporal trends in development near focal-species nest clusters.

We calculated means and variances summarizing distances to, and densities of, roads and wells (distinguishing established and new wells) in relation to known raptor nest clusters for each year of the relevant monitoring periods. We calculated and examined both species-specific and combined-species summary statistics, and used simple analysis of variance (ANOVA) or regression analyses to discern patterns of variation across years. We designed this basic approach to demonstrate how the proximity and density of wells changed at raptor nest clusters over the monitoring period. In addition to providing a thumbnail sketch of overall development patterns, this information also shed light on any relationships (or lack thereof) between development and nest-cluster activity revealed by subsequent analyses. We also prepared and examined GIS-based maps displaying the distributions of wells and roads by year to investigate spatial patterns of development over time.

Objective 2: Describe distributional patterns of nest cluster status in relation to development hotspots.

We used GIS to compare the spatial arrangement of species-specific nest clusters in relation to breeding status and development activities over time. We focused our assessment on the period 1998–2006 in both study areas. This period encompassed all primary survey years in Price and the most suitable survey period in Rawlins. Data inspection revealed limited survey efforts in Rawlins between 1993 and 1997, especially for species other than the Ferruginous Hawk (e.g., only 2–9 Golden Eagle and 0–3 Prairie Falcon nests were surveyed each year during this period). The period prior to this gap also was largely unsuited to this analysis due to initial lower survey efforts and fewer known nests. We identified development "hotspots" as areas with 2006 well densities >0.6 per km^2 (or the equivalent of >1.2 wells within a 0.8-km radius), but also continual additional OG development since 1998. From these identified hotspots, we selected all areas containing at least five identifiable raptor nest clusters with five or more years of survey history between 1998 and 2006. We selected this criterion to meet minimum sample size needs and survey consistency needs to detect long-term patterns in species' activity histories. However, five years may well be an inadequate period to ensure effective representation of Golden Eagle nesting histories, given that individual pairs may not breed every year (Kochert et al. 2002).

Next, we used ArcGIS Spatial Analyst to quantify interannual distances between clusters of differing breeding status (see definitions below) and centers of development activity. We derived development center points in the GIS from the mean center location of 1998 active wells within each selected hotspot (i.e., to serve as a static "initial conditions" reference point). In classifying the breeding status of nests and nest clusters for purposes of the above analyses, we used two overlapping classification scenarios to account for status-classification uncertainties inherent in both study-area datasets, and conducted separate analyses to evaluate whether or not the two classification scenarios yielded different results:

(1) "Used" = evidence of recent nest tending, occupation, or actual breeding attempt obtained

"Unused" = no such evidence obtained, despite nest check

(2) "Active" = breeding attempt confirmed

"Other" = all other cases, including some used (i.e., evidence of tending, but not actual breeding) and all unused classifications

It is important to note that the used vs. unused classification scheme was relatively loose in regards to "positive" status classifications (i.e., used or active), while the active versus other classification scheme was more restrictive, comparing only clusters with verified breeding attempts against all other clusters. For example, evidence of tending was much more subjective than that of actual

breeding attempts. We adopted this dual classification approach in an attempt to strike a balance between maximum "positive" sample sizes (used vs. unused scheme) and minimum "false positive" classifications (active vs. other scheme).

Because distances between individual nest clusters and hotspot centers varied in relation to the availability of nesting sites within each hotspot, we chose to standardize distances by individual hotspot (i.e., by the mean and standard deviation of distances obtained in each hotspot). We then compared the average standardized distance to used versus unused and active versus other nest clusters relative to hotspot centers on an annual basis. We used the output to describe relative spatial distribution patterns of nest-cluster status over time in areas subjected to significant and expanding OG development activities.

Here it is important to note that evaluating the spatial arrangement of all nest clusters over time was problematic, because the numbers of previously unknown nests detected during each additional survey year by itself produced an apparent increasing density of nest clusters. For example, in 2005, 42 previously unknown (at least in the context of the 1998–2006 database provided by the UDWR) Golden Eagle nests were added to the Price FO raptor database, with few if any of these representing newly constructed nests. In addition, note that the output produced during the pursuit of Objectives 1 and 2 did not provide insight into actual nest-cluster densities, because the distribution of all nest clusters was not known.

For Wyoming Ferruginous Hawks, we also compared the overall distribution of active nests before 1988 and after 1989 to illustrate distributional shifts related to availability of 105 ANSs beginning in 1988. To do this, we used the Kernel Density Estimator tool in ArcGIS Spatial Analyst to calculate kernel densities of active Ferruginous Hawk nests, using a 5-km-radius spatial window, for the periods 1970–1987 and 1990–2006, and developed graphical comparisons of the indicated distributional patterns.

Objective 3: Assess relationships between nest-cluster status and development.

a) Describe development patterns near nest clusters.— We used principal components analysis (PCA; Jongman et al. 1987) to describe general patterns in human-related development near all focal-species nest clusters at the 0.8 and 2.0-km-radius spatial scales. We performed each scale-dependent PCA on seven original development variables calculated in a GIS for all surveyed nest clusters for each year of the study period. The original variables were distance to nearest road, distance to nearest OG well, total length of primary, secondary, and OG roads within 0.8 and 2.0 km, and total count of established and new wells within 0.8 and 2.0 km. PCA reduced the suite of development variables down to a limited number of orthogonal (i.e., uncorrelated) principal components or "development factors" (DFs) to be used in subsequent analyses incorporating a larger suite of potential variables (i.e., development, vegetation, and climate variables). Such data reduction serves to reduce the potential risk of model overfitting (i.e., entering too many parameters relative to available sample sizes) and simplifies interpretation of model results. Additionally, because we expected a priori that correlations would exist between selected individual development variables (e.g., distance to well and density of wells), the production of simplified, orthogonal development factors was appropriate prior to proceeding with more complicated analyses. We described the individual DFs produced for each study area and spatial scale based on original development variable loadings on each factor (Jongman et al. 1987). Additionally, we entered the original development variables calculated annually for each surveyed nest cluster into the PCA equations to produce year-specific, individual nest-cluster DF scores.

b) Annual nest cluster activity.—Once we calculated the DF scores, we began with relatively simple species-specific logistic regression analyses (Hosmer and Lemeshow 1989, Agresti 1990) to identify associations between the breeding status of nest clusters and DFs ("development-only" models). For Rawlins Ferruginous Hawks, we conducted separate analyses for non-ANS and ANS nest clusters, so that in the first case we derived results comparable to those for other species and that provided insight unencumbered by the confounding influence of ANSs, and in the second case so we could compare results for the two suites of nests. We used this initial analysis as a first cut to determine if strong relationships appeared to exist between the breeding status of species-specific nest clusters and the level of surrounding development, independent of considering other possible confounding factors (i.e., vegetation and climatic variation).

Next, we used PCA to simplify the original suites of vegetation variables calculated within 2.0 km of each Price and Rawlins cluster centroid into a lesser series of orthogonal "vegetation factors" (VFs). Although each cluster was represented only once in the initial PCA, we entered the original vegetation variables calculated for each year-specific cluster activity or centroid location into the resulting PCA equations to produce year-specific VF scores for each nest cluster. In this way, we reduced

the original, large (19–22 variables) vegetation datasets to 6 or 7 more manageable vegetation factors to be used in subsequent data analyses (again, serving to reduce the danger of model overfitting and simplify model interpretation).

We then proceeded to more complex multiple logistic regression analyses to further discern species-specific relationships between the annual breeding status of nest clusters (i.e., a binomial response variable defined in various ways [see below]) and OG development levels, while simultaneously accounting for the potential influence of vegetation and climate. These "development-plus" models took the following form:

> Annual Nest Cluster Breeding Status = Development (DF) PC Scores + Vegetation (VF) PC Scores + Annual Climate Indexes + Interaction Terms + Error

Note that this approach required us to assume that the activity status of individual nest clusters could be considered independent from year to year, as the same nest cluster could be entered into the model more than once. Although we recognize the weakness of this assumption (i.e., among the raptor species of interest here, the same breeding pair may use the same nest cluster in multiple years and therefore a given year's outcome may depend on the pair's previous experiences at that site), we felt that the inconsistent surveying of individual nests on a yearly basis minimized the influence of potential autocorrelation among nest clusters across years. The fact that development levels changed annually in each study area lent further credence to this approach. Regardless, we assessed the independence of the errors produced by various permutations of the model to determine the degree to which autocorrelation was an issue. As in Objective 2, we used two overlapping classification scenarios to account for status-classification uncertainties inherent in both study-area datasets (i.e., used/unused and active/other), and conducted separate analyses to evaluate whether or not the two classification scenarios yielded different results. We considered modeling of annual climate variables a substitute for including "year" as a main effect or blocking factor in the analyses.

We used stepwise variable selection procedures and consideration of Akaike's information criterion (AICc) scores to identify the most robust and parsimonious model(s) (Burnham and Anderson 2002). Using iterative forward and backward addition of variables with $P = 0.15$ used as the selection criteria to enter or remove specific variables, we first identified all potential significant models in the following model groups: 1) development only, 2) vegetation only, 3) climate only, 4) and vegetation–climate only. We next inspected the top performing models from these model groups to guide the creation of more complex models of development in combination with vegetation and climate variables ("development-plus" models). We used automatic forward and backward selection procedures to identify additional significant models not suggested by the component group models. At each step of model building in this more complex framework, and where sample sizes allowed for it, we inspected the significance of DF x VF and DF x climate-variable interactions in the presence of relevant main effects.

We then evaluated all significant group and combination models with AICc. We chose to use AICc because we were evaluating some models (e.g., Price Prairie Falcons) with small sample sizes. AICc is recommended for small sample sizes, but produces nearly identical results when sample sizes are large (Burnham and Anderson 2002). For each species and study area, we considered the top models (i.e., the most likely models, given the data under consideration) to be those with values of $\Delta AICc < 4$ (Burnham and Anderson 2002). We also calculated Hosmer–Lemeshow goodness-of-fit tests (Hosmer and Lemeshow 1989) to evaluate whether or not the top-ranked model represented a significant fit to the data, and specifically draw attention in the results section to those cases where poor fit was suggested. For each species, we present the top models and log-likelihood values, $\Delta AICc$ values, and associated Akaike weights (w_i; i.e., the probability of a model given the data) for each model.

Although model averaging is a popular method for summarizing the top models identified by AIC (e.g., see Burnham and Anderson 2002), our model building procedures precluded this approach. We allowed our models to contain development variables measured at either or both of the 0.8 and 2.0-km spatial scales, and occasionally found that the relationship of cluster status to a particular development factor measured at the 2-km scale changed sign in the presence of the same development factor measured at the 0.8-km scale. This was because the 2-km scale encompassed the information captured at the 0.8-km scale, but also additional information. Given this reality, model averaging had the potential to obscure the actual relationships revealed by the individual top models.

c) **Proportional nest-cluster use and activity.**—We used multiple regression (Sokal and Rohlf 1995) to analyze relationships between species-specific, proportional nest-cluster "use" and "activity" rates (i.e., the proportion of survey years in which a nest cluster was "used" or "active" [as defined above]) and OG development levels,

while accounting for other potentially confounding factors. For this analysis, we limited consideration to those clusters surveyed for a minimum of five consecutive years during the survey period of interest (1998–2006). For Rawlins Ferruginous Hawks, we limited these analyses to consideration of only non-ANS nest clusters. Because the response variables were derived from multiple years of data gathered from the same nest clusters, it was necessary to account for the potential variation in development and vegetation metrics that may have occurred during the survey years. For example, development metrics associated with a particular nest cluster could change from year to year due to actual changes in development levels or from shifting use of different nests within the cluster. In contrast, variation in vegetation metrics from one year to the next could only result from shifting nest use within a cluster (i.e., because the vegetation layer used in our analyses was static). In order to more accurately reflect the development and vegetation patterns at each nest cluster, we chose to average the DF and VF PCA scores obtained from each year a nest cluster was surveyed between 1998–2006. Additionally, we calculated the variance associated with the DF scores from each nest cluster to reflect the amount of change in development that occurred during the years of survey. Therefore, the models took the form:

Proportional Nest Cluster Use or Activity = Average DF Scores + Variance of DF Scores + Average VF Scores + Interaction Terms + Error

Note that because the datum of interest in this analysis was calculated across a standardized period for all nest clusters, we did not account for annual environmental-condition variables as in (b) above. For these species-specific analyses, we adopted similar variable and model selection and diagnostic procedures as outlined in (b) above.

This was the only tool at our disposal to investigate whether development activities affected the long-term activity status of individual nest clusters.

Objective 4: Assess Ferruginous Hawk nest success and productivity in relation to development.

Only Wyoming Ferruginous Hawks were surveyed adequately to provide robust nest-cluster sample sizes for which nesting success and productivity were determined. Similar to the approach outlined for Objective 3 above, we began by formulating relatively simple logistic regression (nesting success) or linear regression (productivity) analyses that incorporated only data from non-ANS nest clusters and used DF scores as the predictor variables. We then proceeded to analyze more complex multiple logistic and linear regression models that included both non-ANS and ANS nests and incorporated other environmental covariates similar to those modeled under Objective 3b, plus additional substrate/accessibility predictors. Note that the same issues outlined above concerning possible problems with lack of independence between repeat measures of activity at the same nest cluster applied here.

Objective 5: Assess the response of Ferruginous Hawks to artificial nest structures.

Accomplishing this objective entailed summarizing additional insight derived from Neal (2007) concerning how Ferruginous Hawks in the Wyoming study area responded over time to the availability of natural-gas condensation tanks as nesting substrate and their subsequent responses to installation of ANSs to reduce such occurrences. Preliminary evidence suggested that installation of natural-gas condensation tanks initially provided Ferruginous Hawks with attractive nesting opportunities in an area largely lacking other vertically raised nesting structures. Although hard data testifying to this fact were not collected, we presumed that novel, secure nest sites located in areas rich in prey resources were the primary attractor in this context. We designed the analyses outlined above to help us discern if use of ANSs translated to different responses to OG development compared to use of natural nest substrates. Preliminary investigations further suggested that use of ANSs resulted in noticeable alterations of the species' ecology relative to sensitivity to human disturbance, use and maintenance of alternate nest sites, allocation of adult effort toward nest protection/vigilance versus foraging, and susceptibility of nests to mammalian predation. As part of his thesis work, Neal collected additional data to help highlight the nature of these factors and responses. For example, he compared the average number of alternate nests in nest clusters pre- and post-ANS availability, with the evidence suggesting that availability of ANSs resulted in a substantial reduction in the use of alternate nests over time. Second, he collected 299 hours of observational data at 25 natural nests and 25 ANSs to quantify differences in nest attendance and prey-delivery rates. Third, he amassed a few dozen observations testifying to occurrence of mammalian predation as a significant cause of adult and nestling mortality at accessible natural nests, with predation of any kind rarely occurring at inaccessible ANSs or natural nests.

Price, Utah Study Area

Objective 1: Describe temporal trends in development near focal-species nest clusters.

The total length of all roads within the Price study area increased only slightly from 14,210 km in 1998 to 14,375 km in 2006. The change was due entirely to an increase in the total length of OG roads added annually in association with newly developed wells (i.e., 1,432 km of OG roads in 1998 vs. 1,597 km in 2006). The total number of OG wells increased much more dramatically from 451 to 1,177 between 1998 and 2006. The greatest addition of new wells occurred between 1999 and 2002 (Figure 3). Similarly, the average number of wells within 0.8 and 2.0 km of Golden Eagle, Red-tailed Hawk, and Prairie Falcon nest-cluster centroids (n = 264) increased most dramatically from 1999 to 2002 (Figure 4). The average distance to the nearest road relative to 264 identifiable raptor nest clusters (including Golden Eagles, Red-tailed Hawks, and Prairie Falcons), as well as the total length of roads within 0.8 km and 2.0 km of nest clusters did not change significantly between 1998 and 2006 (Table 1). It is important to note, however, that these results likely are confounded by incomplete representation of road-development histories, in that the road layer we worked with did not reflect changes in non-OG roads between 1998 and 2006 (i.e., classification of non-OG roads reflected only the 2006 scene, not year-specific scenes, and once assigned the classification by type of individual road segments remained static across all years). In contrast to the above results, the average distance to the nearest well decreased significantly and the average number of wells within 0.8 and 2.0 km

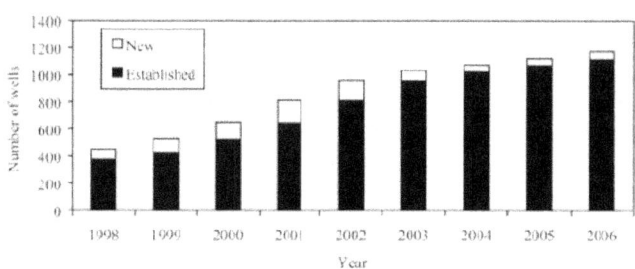

Figure 3. Total number of new and established oil and gas wells found in the Price, Utah study area between 1998 and 2006.

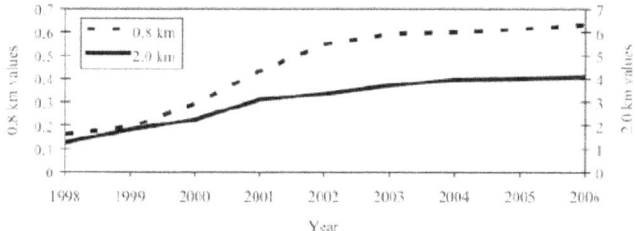

Figure 4. Average numbers of active oil and gas wells within 0.8 and 2.0 km of 264 raptor nest-cluster centroids in the Price, Utah study area from 1998 to 2006.

increased significantly between 1998 and 2006 (Table 1). Between 1998 and 2006, the average distance to a well decreased by 1.2 km, while the average numbers of wells within 0.8 and 2.0 km of relevant nest clusters increased three and four fold, respectively (Table 1). Additionally, the maximum number of wells proximate to nest clusters increased from four to six at the 0.8-km-radius scale and from 17 to 27 at the 2.0-km-radius scale. Over this same period, the overall percentage of nest clusters with no wells nearby declined ~19% at both the 0.8-km and 2.0-km scales (Table 2); however, further investigation revealed substantial variation in this reduction factor

Table 1. Comparison (univariate t-tests) of 1998 and 2006 well and road metrics near 264 raptor nest clusters (including Golden Eagles, Red-tailed Hawks, and Prairie Falcons) in the Price, Utah study area.

Variable	1998		2006		
	Mean	SE	Mean	SE	P
Distance to nearest road (km)	0.58	0.029	0.57	0.028	0.718
Length of road within 0.8 km (km)	1.43	0.084	1.52	0.088	0.467
Length of road within 2.0 km (km)	11.66	0.413	12.48	0.457	0.186
Distance to nearest well (km)	5.30	0.273	4.08	0.274	0.002
Number of wells within 0.8 km	0.16	0.034	0.63	0.072	<0.001
Number of wells within 2.0 km	1.25	0.192	4.08	0.427	<0.001

Table 2. Percentages of 264 raptor nest clusters (including Golden Eagles, Red-tailed Hawks, and Prairie Falcons) with oil and gas wells within 0.8 and 2.0 km of cluster centroids in the Price, Utah study area in 1998 and 2006.

	Within 0.8 km			Within 2.0 km	
# Wells	1998	2006	# Wells	1998	2006
0	90.2%	70.8%	0	73.1%	54.2%
1	5.3%	11.4%	1	8.7%	8.3%
2	3.0%	6.1%	2-5	9.5%	14.0%
3	1.1%	8.3%	6-10	4.9%	6.8%
4	0.4%	2.7%	11-15	2.7%	3.0%
5	0.0%	0.4%	16-20	1.1%	8.0%
6	0.0%	0.4%	>20	0.0%	5.7%

Table 3. Percentages by land owner/manager of 264 raptor nest clusters (including Golden Eagles, Red-tailed Hawks, and Prairie Falcons) with no gas or oil wells within 0.8 and 2.0 km of cluster centroids in 1998 and 2006 in the Price, Utah study area.

Land Manager	n	Within 0.8 km		Within 2.0 km	
		1998	2006	1998	2006
BLM	107	89%	66%	74%	49%
USFS	48	98%	98%	85%	83%
State	46	83%	41%	59%	26%
Private	63	92%	79%	73%	62%

depending on land ownership. The percentages of nest clusters with no wells within 0.8 km and 2.0 km declined by roughly 25% at both scales on BLM lands, and declined the most on state lands (42% decline within 0.8 km; 33% decline with 2.0 km; Table 3). Due to the concentrated nature of OG development in the Price study area, most nest clusters in areas of energy development were proximate to multiple wells. For example, by 2006, 61% of all identifiable nest clusters near wells had two or more wells within 0.8 km of cluster centroids, and 70% had five or more wells within 2.0 km of cluster centroids

Objective 2: Describe distributional patterns of nest cluster status in relation to development hotspots.

We identified three OG development hotspots in the Price study area that met our screening criteria (Figure 5). Within these hotspots, we identified 43 Golden Eagle, 14 Red-tailed Hawk, and 3 Prairie Falcon nest clusters that met our screening criteria. To be considered, we required a species to have at least five nest clusters per year represented in both the "used" and "unused" or "active" and "other" status categories (see the Glossary for a description of each category), which limited the comparison to Golden Eagles with clusters classified as used and unused. Relative to the hotspot center locations (with distances standardized based on within-hotspot averages), the average standardized distance

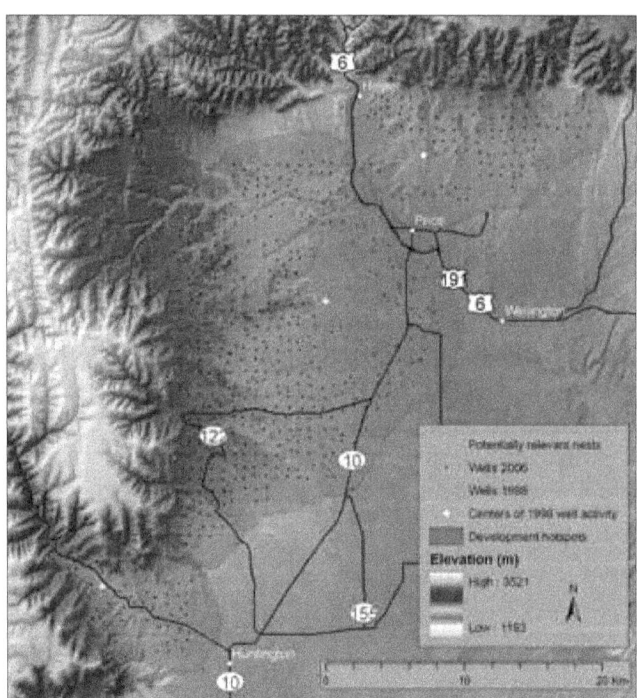

Figure 5. Map depicting the distribution of raptor nests from nest clusters with ≥5 years of survey history between 1998 and 2006 within three oil and gas development "hotspots" in the Price, Utah study area.

to used Golden Eagle nests ($n = 204$, mean = 0.03 ± 0.07 standardized units) was greater than the average distance to unused nests ($n = 209$, mean = -0.02 ± 0.07 standardized units), but the difference was not significant

($t = -0.53$, df = 411, $P = 0.60$). A plot of average standardized distances to used versus unused nests by year further suggested, however, that used nests were consistently farther from development centers from 2000 through 2003, the period of most intensive development (Figure 6).

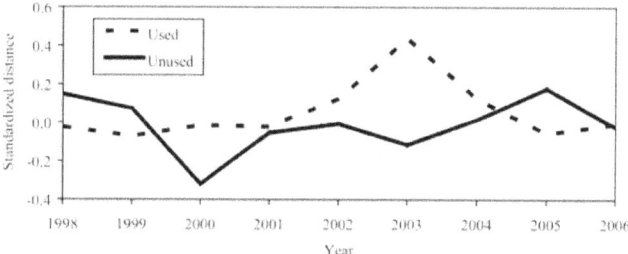

Figure 6. Average standardized distance between development "hotspot" centers and used and unused Golden Eagle nest clusters in the Price, Utah study area from 1998 to 2006.

Objective 3: Assess relationships between nest cluster status and development.

a) Describe development patterns near nest clusters.— The PCAs identified two principal components with eigenvalues >1.0 at both the 0.8 and 2.0-km spatial scales. The first two PCs explained 57% of the variance in the 0.8-km dataset and 58% of the variance in the

2.0-km dataset, and the relevant component loadings yielded similar interpretations at both scales (Figure 7). The first PC, or development factor 1 (DF1), contrasts OG development levels; i.e., moving right along DF1 is primarily associated with increasing total length of OG roads, increasing densities of established and new wells, and decreasing distances to the nearest wells and roads. The second PC (DF2) contrasts non-OG roads levels; i.e., moving up along DF2 is primarily associated with increasing total length of secondary and primary roads, and decreasing distance to roads. The fact that distance to road appears in both DF1 and DF2 suggests that decreasing distance to the nearest road is a characteristic common to both high levels of OG development and non-OG roads near raptor nest clusters. Given the straightforward interpretation and high congruence between PCs produced at each scale, we chose to use DF1 and DF2 scores in place of individual development variables in subsequent analyses.

b) Annual nest-cluster activity.—Initial species-specific analyses of nest-cluster status (with the dependent variable as "used/unused" or "active/other") versus DF1 and DF2 (i.e., logistic regression without inclusion of vegetation and climatic variables) revealed significant relationships between development and the activity status of nest clusters. For Golden Eagles, the analyses indicated negative relationships between DF1 and cluster "use" at both scales and cluster "activity" at the 0.8-km

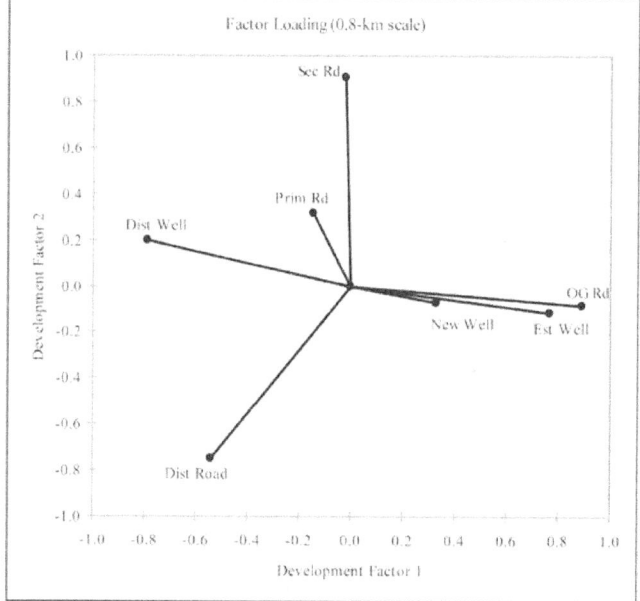

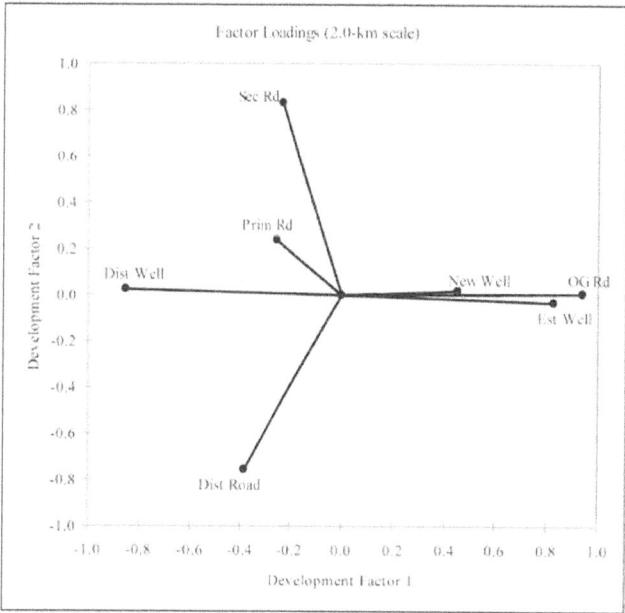

Figure 7. Graphical display of individual development-variable loadings associated with two primary development factors identified by Principal Components Analysis of characteristics associated with 264 raptor nest clusters at the 0.8-km and 2.0-km radius spatial scales in the Price, Utah study area.

scale (i.e., use or activity was greater in areas with less OG development). In contrast DF2 related positively to cluster use at the 2-km scale and cluster activity at both scales (i.e., use and activity were greater in areas with more non-OG roads). For Red-tailed Hawks, the probability of cluster use or activity related positively to OG development at the 0.8-km scale, but related negatively to it at the 2.0-km scale. Cluster use also related positively to non-OG roads at the 0.8 km scale, but not at the larger scale. No significant relationships were indicated for Prairie Falcons.

PCA of the proportional coverage of 22 original landcover/vegetation variables within a 2-km radius of nest clusters produced seven PCs with eigenvalues >1.0, which collectively explained 68% of the variation in the dataset (Table 4). It is important to note that we created these vegetation factors to account for the potential confounding influence vegetation may have on nest-cluster status in subsequent models and to assess how

vegetation modified relationships with development. Therefore, it is not our intention to provide detailed interpretations of cluster status/vegetation relationships. That said, the first PC, labeled VF1, accounted for 19.6% of the total variance and involved a contrast between primarily clusters dominated by mixes of pinyon-juniper, desert shrub, and Wyoming big sagebrush, and those dominated by mixes of conifer, aspen-mix forest, mountain big sagebrush, and mountain shrub cover (i.e., for the most part reflecting an elevational gradient). VF2 accounted for an additional 13.6% of the total variance and further distinguished between primarily clusters dominated by pinyon, juniper, and mixed-species sagebrush cover, and those dominated by mountain and basin big sagebrush. VF3 accounted for an additional 9.7% of the total variance and further distinguished primarily clusters dominated by riparian forest, grass, forbs, and black sagebrush. VF4 accounted for an additional 8.0% of the total variance and further distinguished primarily clusters dominated by pinyon,

Table 4. Summary of Principal Components Analysis describing seven primary landcover/vegetation factors with eigenvalues >1.0 derived from 22 original landcover/vegetation variables representing proportional coverage within 2 km of 264 raptor nest clusters in the Price, Utah study area (asterisks indicate high loadings that comprise the primary variables involved in each factor).

Land cover variables	Land Cover Factors Produced by Principal Components Analysis						
	1	2	3	4	5	6	7
Grass	0.151	-0.431	0.508*	0.051	-0.107	-0.277	0.099
Forb	0.449	0.104	0.567*	0.189	-0.166	0.069	-0.294
Sagebrush general	0.153	-0.723*	-0.371	-0.164	0.106	-0.026	-0.049
Wyoming big sagebrush	-0.677*	0.416	0.019	0.119	-0.013	0.002	-0.315*
Mountain big sagebrush	0.538*	0.552*	-0.041	-0.193	-0.163	0.127	0.183
Basin big sagebrush	-0.322	0.516*	-0.146	0.121	-0.153	0.219	-0.238
Black sagebrush	0.213	0.139	0.595*	0.002	-0.517*	0.044	0.125
Rabbitbrush	-0.220	0.288	0.169	0.204	0.479*	0.233	0.296
Desert shrub	-0.572*	-0.242	0.345	-0.505*	-0.044	-0.098	0.004
Riparian shrub	0.372	0.184	0.002	-0.305	0.391	-0.368*	-0.383*
Riparian forest	-0.027	0.000	0.556*	0.062	0.462*	0.123	0.072
Mountain shrub	0.744*	0.309	0.139	0.058	-0.099	0.313	0.070
Oak-maple	0.395	0.440	-0.444	-0.215	0.058	0.089	0.396*
Aspen mix	0.673*	0.271	0.000	-0.239	0.226	-0.272	-0.242
Conifer	0.778*	-0.040	-0.152	0.303	0.222	-0.043	0.050
Pinyon-juniper	-0.673*	0.066	-0.177	0.512*	-0.115	-0.089	0.084
Pinyon	0.289	-0.513*	-0.280	0.429*	0.044	0.090	-0.033
Juniper	0.023	-0.662*	-0.105	-0.273	-0.002	0.457*	-0.012
Barren	0.488	-0.442	0.224	0.460*	-0.057	-0.101	0.071
Water	0.125	-0.069	0.026	0.144	0.153	0.546*	-0.515*
Agriculture	-0.090	-0.208	0.270	-0.486*	0.121	0.346*	0.116
Human habitation	-0.314	0.113	0.317	0.211	0.582*	-0.025	0.177
Cumulative variance explained	19.6%	33.2%	42.9%	50.9%	57.6%	63.1%	68.0%

pinyon-juniper mix, and barren lands from those dominated by desert shrub and agricultural habitats. VF5 accounted for an additional 6.3% of the total variance and further distinguished primarily clusters dominated by black sagebrush from those dominated by rabbitbrush, riparian forest, and human habitations. VF6 accounted for an additional 5.5% of the total variance and further distinguished primarily clusters dominated by juniper, water, and agricultural habitats, with a weak contrast against clusters with relatively high representation of riparian shrub cover. Finally, VF7 accounted for an additional 4.9% of the total variance and further distinguished primarily clusters associated with a relatively high degree of open water and to lesser degrees riparian shrub and Wyoming big sagebrush, with a weak contrast against clusters with relatively high oak-maple cover.

An initial graphical examination of relationships between the probability of clusters being active in May and climatic variables suggested possible correlations (Figure 8). In particular, activity levels appeared to track PDSI during the previous year (PDSI_lyr) fairly well, with relatively high correlations between these parameters for Prairie Falcons (0.69) and Golden Eagles (0.67), but a weaker relationship for Red-tailed Hawks (0.36). Additionally, the probability of nests being active

declined markedly for all three focal species during the worst drought years of 2002 and 2003, but quickly improved again as moisture conditions began to rebound in the following years.

Adding landcover/vegetation and climatic variables to the models revealed additional complexity, with all best-fitting models including one or more landcover/vegetation factors and, with one exception, one or more annual climatic variables (Tables 5–12).

With the seven VFs and climate variables incorporated as potential covariates along with the four DFs as predictors, we identified six top models that helped explain differences between "used" ($n = 534$ events) and "unused" ($n = 569$) Golden Eagle nest clusters (Table 5). Top models (i.e., the most likely models, given the data under consideration) were identified as those with ΔAICc values <4.0. Although the top models varied slightly, they revealed underlying vegetation, climate, and development relationships. Inspection of actual model coefficients suggested that nest cluster use related positively to DF2_2K, VF2, PDSI, and PDSI_lyr, and related negatively to DF1_0.8K, DF1_2K, VF5, and VF7. In addition, five of the six top models contained an interaction between VF5 and DF1. These results suggest that the probability of a Golden Eagle nest

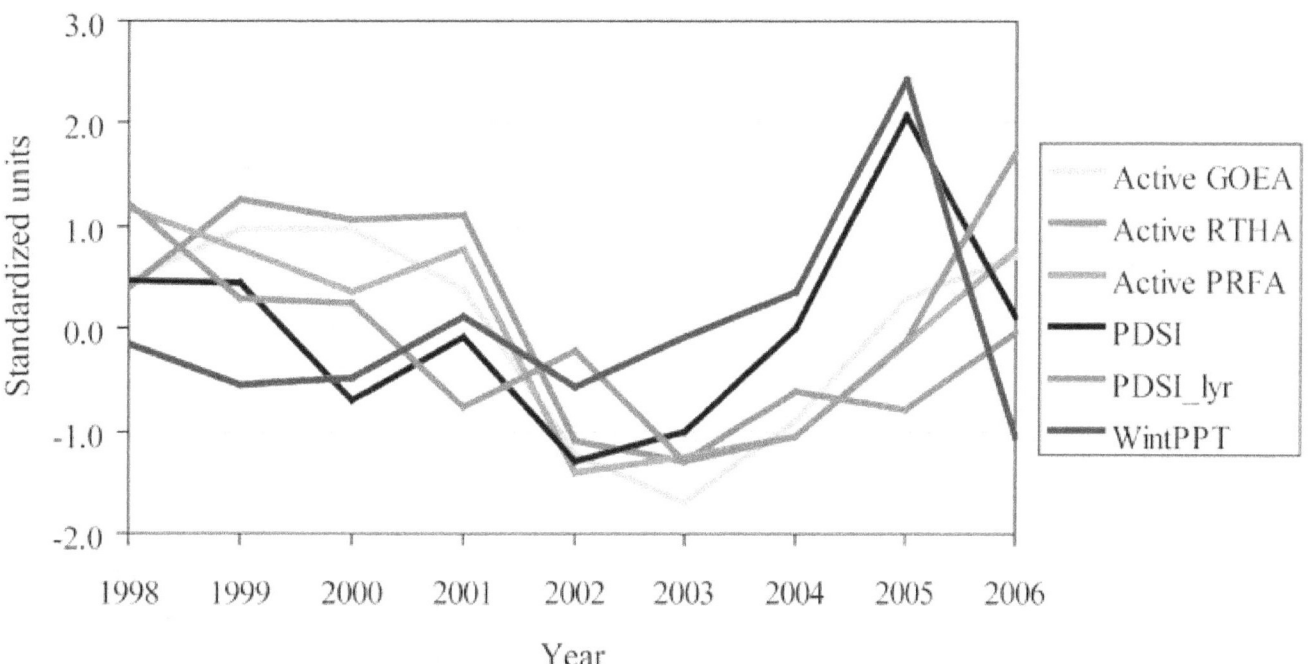

Figure 8. Comparison of trends in annual, species-specific, proportional nest-cluster activity, the Palmer Drought Severity Index (PDSI; higher values = less drought severity), PDSI in the previous year (PDSI_lyr), and winter precipitation (WintPPT) in the Price, Utah study area from 1998–2006. All measures have been standardized for direct comparison.

cluster being used in a given year generally increased as overall development activity decreased and where the prevalence of non-OG roads was relatively high at the 2-km scale. However, a significant interaction between DF1 and VF5 in five of the six top models also indicated that the negative influence of expanding development was particularly enhanced in areas with human habitations, cover of rabbitbrush, and/or riparian forest, but shifted to a positive relationship in habitats with high cover of black sagebrush. Otherwise, the results for VF2 suggested that the probability of cluster use increased as the proportion of mountain and basin big sagebrush cover within 2 km of the cluster increased and declined as the proportion of pinyon, juniper, and mixed-species sagebrush cover increased. The significance of VF7 further suggested that the probability of cluster use also increased in habitats with a relatively high degree of open water (i.e., in clusters located near the prominent reservoirs in the study area: Joe's Valley Reservoir and

those in Huntington Canyon). Drought severity during the current year (PDSI) and previous year (PDSI_lyr) also significantly influenced the probability of cluster use, with use declining with increasing drought severity.

We identified four top models that helped explain differences between "active" ($n = 312$ events) and "other" ($n = 791$) Golden Eagle nest clusters (Table 6). These models suggested that nest-cluster activity related positively to DF2_2K, VF2, and PDSI, and related negatively to DF1_0.8K, DF1_2K, VF4, VF5, and WintPPT (Table 6). Similar to the "use" models above, an interaction between DF1 (0.8 or 2.0-km scale) and VF5 also was identified in the top "activity" models. The top activity and use models revealed similar relationships with both DF1 and DF2. Overall, both the use and activity models suggested that the probability of a Golden Eagle cluster being used or active in May increased as overall OG development activity decreased proximate

Table 5. Top multiple logistic regression models (ΔAICc <4.0) describing the relationships between the probability of a Golden Eagle nest cluster being "used" in a given year and various oil and gas development factors (DFs), landcover/vegetation factors (VFs), and climate variables in the Price, Utah study area.

Development Factors	Vegetation Factors	Climate Factors	Interactions	K	Log(L)	ΔAICc	w_i
DF1_0.8K, DF2_2K	VF2, VF5, VF6, VF7	PDSI, PDSI_lyr	DF1_0.8K*VF5, DF2_2K*VF6	11	-727.93	0.00	0.28
DF1_0.8K, DF2_2K	VF2, VF5, VF6, VF7	PDSI, PDSI_lyr	DF2_2K*VF6	10	-729.30	0.70	0.20
DF1_2K	VF2, VF5, VF7	PDSI, PDSI_lyr	D1_2K*VF5	8	-731.89	1.80	0.11
DF1_2K	VF2, VF5, VF7	PDSI, WintPPT	DF1_2K*VF5	8	-732.28	2.58	0.08
DF1_0.8K, DF2_2K	VF2, VF5, VF7	PDSI, PDSI_lyr	DF1_0.8K*VF5, DF2_2K*PDSI	11	-729.76	3.67	0.04
DF1_0.8K	VF2, VF5, VF7	PDSI, PDSI_lyr	DF1_0.8K*F5, DF1_0.8K*VF7, D1_0.8K*PDSI_lyr	10	-730.86	3.82	0.04

Note: K = number of parameters, including constant and error terms; Log(L) = log likelihood; w_i = Akaike's weight, indicating probability of model given the data (Burnham and Anderson 2002).

Table 6. Top multiple logistic regression models (ΔAICc <4.0) describing relationships between the probability of a Golden Eagle nest cluster being "active" in a given year and oil and gas development factors (DFs), landcover/vegetation factors (VFs), and climate variables in the Price, Utah study area.

Development Factors	Vegetation Factors	Climate Factors	Interactions	K	Log(L)	ΔAICc	w_i
DF1_2K	VF1, VF2, VF4, VF5	PDSI, WintPPT	DF1_2K*VF5	9	-606.74	0.00	0.43
DF1_0.8K	VF1, VF2, VF4, VF5	PDSI, WintPPT	DF1_0.8K*VF5	10	-606.94	2.44	0.13
DF1_2K, DF2_2K	VF2, VF4, VF5	PDSI, WintPPT	DF1_2K*VF5	9	-608.04	2.60	0.12
DF1_2K	VF2, VF4, VF5	PDSI, WintPPT	DF1_2K*VF5	8	-609.25	2.99	0.10

Note: K = number of parameters, including constant and error terms; Log(L) = log likelihood; w_i = Akaike's weight, indicating probability of model given the data (Burnham and Anderson 2002).

to clusters, as the prevalence of non-OG roads increased at the 2.0-km scale, as current-year drought severity decreased, as cover of mountain and basin big sagebrush increased (and pinyon and juniper decreased [VF2]), and as cover of miscellaneous human infrastructure and rabbitbrush decreased and cover of black sagebrush increased (VF5).

A comparison of used (n = 98 events) and unused (n = 119) Red-tailed Hawk nest clusters produced 18 top models with considerable model variation (Table 7). However, some common patterns were evident. The top models commonly revealed that cluster use related positively to DF1_0.8K, DF2_0.8K, VF2, PDSI, and PDSI_lyr, but related negatively to DF1_2K, VF4, and WintPPT. These results suggest that the probability

of Red-tailed Hawk nest clusters being used increased as all types of development increased close to the nest (i.e., within 0.8 km), but decreased as OG development increased in the larger landscape (i.e., within 2.0 km). Additionally, use increased in habitats dominated by a mix of mountain and basin big sagebrush cover, but decreased in habitats dominated by a mix of pinyon, juniper, and mixed-species sagebrush cover. Use also increased as current or prior-year drought severity declined.

We identified only a single top model that helped explain differences between active (n = 72 events) and other (n = 145) Red-tailed Hawk nest clusters (Table 8). The coefficients of this model suggest that cluster activity related positively to DF1_0.8K and VF2, and

Table 7. Top multiple logistic regression models (ΔAICc <4.0) describing the relationships between the probability of a Red-tailed Hawk nest cluster being "used" in a given year and oil and gas development factors (DFs), landcover/vegetation factors (VFs), and climate variables in the Price, Utah study area.

Development Factors	Vegetation Factors	Climate Factors	K	Log(L)	ΔAICc	w_i
DF1_0.8K, DF1_2K	VF2	PDSI_lyr	5	-141.54	0.00	0.13
DF1_0.8K, DF1_2K	VF4	PDSI_lyr	5	-141.72	0.35	0.11
DF1_0.8K, DF1_2K	VF4	None	4	-143.07	0.93	0.08
DF1_0.8K, DF1_2K	VF2	PDSI, WintPPT	6	-141.21	1.46	0.06
DF1_0.8K, DF1_2K	VF4	PDSI, WintPPT	6	-141.32	1.69	0.05
DF1_0.8K, DF1_2K	None	None	3	-144.71	2.11	0.04
None	VF4	PDSI_lyr	3	-144.74	2.17	0.04
DF2_0.8K	VF4	PDSI_lyr	4	-143.75	2.29	0.04
DF1_2K	VF4	PDSI_lyr	4	-143.88	2.56	0.04
DF1_0.8K, DF1_2K	None	PDSI, WintPPT	5	-143.07	3.05	0.03
DF1_0.8K, DF2_0.8K, DF1_2K	None	None	4	-144.17	3.13	0.03
DF2_0.8K	VF4	None	3	-145.26	3.21	0.03
DF1_2K	VF4	None	3	-145.27	3.25	0.02
None	VF4	PDSI, WintPPT	4	-144.24	3.27	0.02
None	VF4	None	2	-146.38	3.38	0.02
DF2_0.8K	VF4	PDSI, WintPPT	5	-143.28	3.48	0.02
None	VF4, VF6	None	3	-145.55	3.79	0.02
None	VF1, VF4	PDSI_lyr	4	-144.51	3.82	0.02

Note: K = number of parameters, including constant and error terms; Log(L) = log likelihood; w_i = Akaike's weight, indicating probability of model given the data (Burnham and Anderson 2002).

Table 8. Top multiple logistic regression model (ΔAICc <4.0) describing the relationships between the probability of a Red-tailed Hawk nest cluster being "active" in a given year and oil and gas development factors (DFs), landcover/vegetation factors (VFs), and climate variables in the Price, Utah study area.

Development Factors	Vegetation Factors	Climate Factors	Interactions	K	Log(L)	ΔAICc	w_i
DF1_0.8K, DF1_2K	VF2, VF3	None	D1_0.8K*VF3	6	-123.42	0.00	0.85

Note: K = number of parameters, including constant and error terms; Log(L) = log likelihood; w_i = Akaike's weight, indicating probability of model given the data (Burnham and Anderson 2002).

negatively related to DF1_2K and VF3. The model also contains a significant interaction between DF1_0.8K and VF3. These results are similar to those derived from the used/unused analysis in suggesting the same mixed relationships with overall development activity at the 0.8 and 2.0-km spatial scales, and relative to the vegetation contrast represented by VF2. These results differ from the used/unused analysis in not representing a significant effect of drought severity and in including a significant interaction between overall development activity at the 0.8-km scale and VF3. The interaction term suggests that the positive effect of increasing, proximate development activity was muted in habitats dominated by mixes of riparian forest, grass, forbs, and oak-maple. The lack of a significant climate term in the active/other model compared to the used/unused model suggests that drought did not affect actual breeding attempts to the same degree.

We identified 13 top models that helped explain differences between used ($n = 34$ events) and unused ($n = 39$) Prairie Falcon nest clusters (Table 9). Due to small sample sizes for this species, we only considered main effects and excluded potential interactions to avoid model overfitting. Overall, these models indicated that Prairie Falcon cluster use related positively to PDSI_1yr or PDSI, and related negatively to DF2_0.8K, DF2_2K, VF3, VF4 (and less commonly VF1 or VF5), and WintPPT. Cluster use related positively to DF1 at the 0.8 or 2.0-km scales when either scale entered a model individually; however, use had a mixed relationship with DF1 when both scales were included in the same model (i.e., a

positive relationship at the 0.8-km scale and negative at 2.0-km). These results suggest that the probability of a Prairie Falcon nest cluster being used increased as OG development increased, but that this effect diminished at the larger landscape scale. In contrast, cluster use increased as prevalence and proximity of non-OG roads decreased at both scales. Cluster use also increased as proportional cover of riparian forest, grass, forbs, and black sagebrush decreased (VF3); increased as the proportional cover of pinyon, pinyon-juniper mix, and barren lands decreased and the proportional cover of desert shrub and agricultural habitats increased (VF4); and increased as prior or current year drought severity declined. Note that we detected no relationships between cluster status and development in prior development-only models.

We identified three top models that helped explain differences between active ($n = 28$ events) and other ($n = 45$) Prairie Falcon nest clusters (Table 10). These models suggested that cluster activity related positively to VF2 and PDSI, and negatively related to DF2_0.8K, VF3, VF4, VF5, VF6, and WintPPT. These results agree with those of the used/unused analysis in suggesting similar relationships with trends in the density and proximity of non-OG roads (although the active models only identified the 0.8-km scale as important). However, the top models of Prairie Falcon cluster activity identified no significant relationships with OG development. The negative relationships between cluster use or activity and VF3 and VF4 also are apparent in all top models (Tables 9 and

Table 9. Top multiple logistic regression models (ΔAICc <4.0) describing relationships between the probability of a Prairie Falcon nest cluster being "used" in a given year and oil and gas development factors (DFs), landcover/vegetation factors (VFs), and climate variables in the Price, Utah study area.

Development Factors	Vegetation Factors	Climate Factors	K	Log(L)	ΔAICc	w_i
DF1_0.8K, DF2_2K	VF3, VF4	PDSI_1yr	6	-34.80	0.00	0.17
DF2_0.8K	VF3, VF4, VF5	PDSI_1yr	6	-34.91	0.20	0.16
DF2_0.8K	VF3, VF4	PDSI_1yr	5	-36.33	0.60	0.13
DF2_2K	VF3, VF4	PDSI_1yr	5	-36.47	0.89	0.11
DF1_0.8K, DF1_2K, DF2_0.8K,	VF2, VF3, VF4, VF5, VF7	PDSI_1yr	10	-30.46	1.91	0.07
DF2_2K	VF1, VF3, VF4	PDSI, WintPPT	7	-34.98	2.88	0.04
DF1_0.8K, DF2_2K	VF3, VF4	PDSI, WintPPT	7	-35.02	2.96	0.04
None	VF3, VF4, VF5	PDSI_1yr	5	-37.51	2.97	0.04
DF2_0.8K	VF3, VF4, VF5	PDSI, WintPPT	7	-35.03	2.97	0.04
DF2_0.8K	VF3, VF4	PDSI, WintPPT	6	-36.35	3.09	0.04
None	VF1, VF3, VF4	PDSI_1yr	5	-37.70	3.35	0.03
DF1_2K, DF2_2K	VF3, VF4	PDSI, WintPPT	7	-35.33	3.58	0.03
DF2_2K	VF3, VF4	PDSI, WintPPT	6	-36.79	3.97	0.02

Note: K = number of parameters, including constant and error terms; Log(L) = log likelihood; w_i = Akaike's weight, indicating probability of model given the data (Burnham and Anderson 2002).

10). Again, these relationships suggest that cluster use or activity increased as proportional cover of riparian forest, grass, forbs, and black sagebrush decreased (VF3), and as the cover of pinyon, pinyon-juniper mix, and barren lands decreased and cover of desert shrub and agricultural habitats increased (VF4). Additionally, all use and activity models suggested a positive response to wetter conditions during either the previous year (PDSI_1yr) or current year (PDSI) as long as winter precipitation was not too high (WintPPT).

c) Proportional nest-cluster activity.—We identified 129 Golden Eagle, 23 Red-tailed Hawk, and 9 Prairie Falcon nest clusters with at least five years of survey history between 1998 and 2006. Limited sample sizes precluded investigating relationships between proportional cluster use or activity and development metrics for other than Golden Eagles. We also modeled only main effects to avoid model overfitting. We identified three top models that helped explain differences in proportional "use" of Golden Eagle nest clusters (i.e., with annual events classified as "used" or "unused"; Table 11). The best model accounted for only 14.7% (adjusted R^2 value) of the total variance in the dependent variable, suggesting that although our modeling identified several important contributors to variation in proportional cluster use, much of the variation remained unexplained. Generally, the models suggested that cluster use related positively to VarDF1_0.8K, VarDF2_0.8K, VF1, and VF2 and negatively related to VF5 and VF7. This suggests that proportional use increased in clusters with high variation in OG levels at the 0.8 km spatial scale. Greater variance in OG development levels could occur either at clusters with large interannual changes in the amount of nearby development or at clusters with multiple, widely spaced alternate nests (i.e., shifting center points from which development metrics were calculated). On the other hand, proportional cluster use increased with variation in the representation of non-OG roads, perhaps reflecting the benefit of large breeding territories with high diversity in non-OG road patterns (perhaps reflecting more nesting options). Note that greater variance in non-OG roads could be driven only by shifting nest use within a cluster across years, because our representation of non-OG roads was static across years. Proportional cluster use also increased in areas of mountain or basin big sagebrush, mountain shrub, conifer, and aspen, and decreased in areas of high pinyon-juniper and Wyoming or mixed-species sagebrush cover (VF1 and VF2); decreased in areas of high human habitation, rabbitbrush, and riparian forest cover and increased in areas of high black sagebrush cover (VF5); and increased in areas with a relatively high proportion of open water (VF7).

Table 10. Top multiple logistic regression models (ΔAICc <4.0) describing the relationships between the probability of a Prairie Falcon nest cluster being "active" in a given year and oil and gas development factors (DFs), landcover/vegetation factors (VFs), and climate variables in the Price, Utah study area.

Development Factors	Vegetation Factors	Climate Factors	K	Log(L)	ΔAICc	w_i
DF2_0.8K	VF2, VF3, VF4, VF5	PDSI, WintPPT	8	-23.37	0.00	0.32
DF2_0.8K	VF2, VF3, VF4, VF5, VF6	PDSI, WintPPT	9	-22.04	0.04	0.31
DF2_0.8K	VF1, VF3, VF4, VF6	PDSI, WintPPT	8	-24.64	2.55	0.09

Note: K = number of parameters, including constant and error terms; Log(L) = log likelihood; w_i = Akaike's weight, indicating probability of model given the data (Burnham and Anderson 2002).

Table 11. Top multiple regression models (ΔAICc <4.0) describing relationships between proportional "use" of Golden Eagle nest clusters (i.e., proportion of years in which evidence of nest tending or breeding was obtained) and oil and gas development factors (DFs; cluster averages and variances) and average landcover/vegetation factors (VFs) in the Price, Utah study area.

Development Factors	Vegetation Factors	K	RSS	ΔAICc	w_i
VarDF1_0.8K, VarDF2_0.8K	VF1, VF5, VF7	6	7.15	0.00	0.54
VarDF2_0.8K	VF1, VF5, VF7	5	7.39	2.00	0.20
VarDF2_0.8K	VF2	3	7.70	2.87	0.13

Note: Top model total R^2 = 18.1%, adjusted R^2 = 14.7%. K = number of parameters, including constant and error terms; RSS = residual sum of squares; w_i = Akaike's weight, indicating probability of model given the data (Burnham and Anderson 2002).

The top two models of proportional nest cluster "activity" (i.e., with annual events classified as "active" or "other"; Table 12) also performed marginally, with the best model accounting for a relatively small proportion of the variance in the dependent variable (adjusted R^2 = 13.1%). The models suggested proportional cluster activity related positively to VarDF1_0.8K or VarDF1_2K and VarDF2_0.8K, and related negatively to VF4. Relationships with development identified by models of use and activity generally were similar. Proportional activity was greater in areas where a high degree of change in overall OG development activity occurred between 1998 and 2006 and/or the diversity of OG development levels across alternate nests within clusters was high at the 0.8 or 2.0-km scales (positive association with VarDF1). In addition, proportional activity was greater in areas where the level of non-OG roads was more diverse across alternate nests within clusters at the 0.8-km scale (i.e., more options?). However, only a single vegetation variable was identified in the proportional activity models, suggesting that activity increased where cover of pinyon-juniper and barren lands within 2 km was low and cover of desert shrub and agricultural habitats was relatively high (VF4 contrast).

Table 12. Top multiple regression models (ΔAICc <4.0) describing relationships between proportional "activity" of Golden Eagle nest clusters (i.e., proportion of years in which a breeding attempt occurred) and oil and gas development factors (DFs; cluster averages and variances) and average landcover/vegetation factors (VFs) in the Price, Utah study area.

Development Factors	Vegetation Factors	K	RSS	ΔAICc	w_i
VarDF1_0.8K, VarDF2_0.8K	VF4	4	4.31	0.00	0.52
VarDF1_2K, VarDF2_0.8K	VF4	4	4.40	2.84	0.13

Note: Top model total R^2 = 15.2%, adjusted R^2 = 13.1%. K = number of parameters, including constant and error terms; RSS = residual sum of squares; w_i = Akaike's weight, indicating probability of model given the data (Burnham and Anderson 2002).

Rawlins, Wyoming Study Area

Objective 1. Describe temporal trends in development near focal-species nest clusters.

The total length of all roads within the Rawlins study area increased slightly from 45,788 km in 1978 to 47,041 km in 2006. The 1,253-km increase solely reflected the addition of OG roads associated with new wells established during this period (4,099 km in 1978 vs. 5,352 km in 2006. The actual change in length of roads during this period was likely larger than these reported values, but our ability to characterize road additions was limited to roads associated with new OG activity. The total number of OG wells in the study area increased from 1,438 to 4,258 between 1978 and 2006. Within this time frame, two distinct periods of increased OG activity occurred: 1978–1985 and 1994–2006 (Figure 9). Similarly, increases in the average number of wells within 0.8 and 2.0 km of Golden Eagle, Ferruginous Hawk, Red-tailed Hawk, and Prairie Falcon nest-cluster

centroids ($n = 1,097$) corresponded roughly to these periods (Figure 10).

A comparison of the average distance to the nearest road and total length of roads proximate to Rawlins nest clusters suggested that only the total length of roads within 2.0 km of cluster centroids differed significantly between 1978 and 2006, increasing by 0.6 km (Table 13). In contrast, all well-related measures changed significantly over this period. The average distance to the nearest well decreased by 1.3 km, while the average number of wells within both 0.8 and 2.0 km increased more than five-fold (Table 13). The maximum number of wells near relevant nest clusters increased from 4 to 13 at the 0.8-km scale and from 20 to 40 at the 2.0-km scale, and the overall proportion of clusters with no wells within 0.8 and 2.0 km decreased by 9% and 12%, respectively (Table 14). Further investigation by land owner/manager revealed slightly larger reductions on BLM-managed lands (12% and 17%) and lower reductions on other lands, with the percentage of clusters with no wells within 2.0 km actually increasing between 1978 and 2006 on state lands (Table 15).

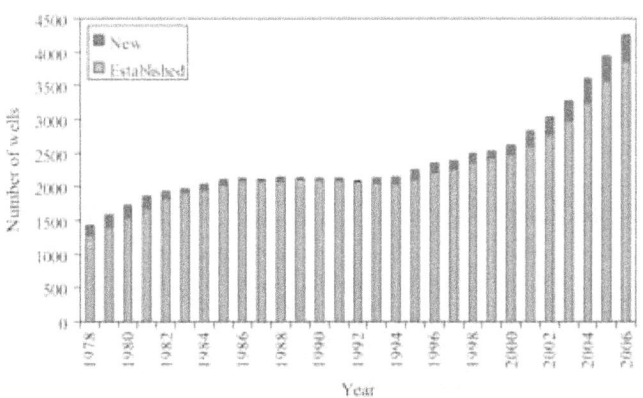

Figure 9. Total number of new and established oil and gas wells found in the Rawlins, Wyoming study area between 1978 and 2006.

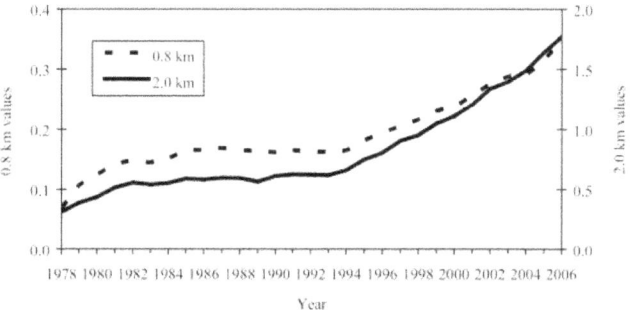

Figure 10. Average numbers of active oil and gas wells within 0.8 and 2.0 km of 1,097 raptor nest-cluster centroids in the Rawlins, Wyoming study area between 1978 and 2006.

Table 13. Comparison (univariate *t*-tests) of 1978 and 2006 well and road metrics near 1,097 raptor nest clusters (including Golden Eagles, Ferruginous Hawks, Red-tailed Hawks, and Prairie Falcons) in the Rawlins, Wyoming study area.

| | 1978 | | 2006 | | |
Variable	Mean	SE	Mean	SE	*P*
Distance to nearest road (km)	0.39	0.011	0.37	0.010	0.258
Length of road within 0.8 km (km)	2.28	0.051	2.36	0.052	0.225
Length of road within 2.0 km (km)	13.98	0.205	14.61	0.213	0.032
Distance to nearest well (km)	6.93	0.177	5.57	0.174	<0.001
Number of wells within 0.8 km	0.07	0.011	0.35	0.041	<0.001
Number of wells within 2.0 km	0.31	0.032	1.77	0.144	<0.001

Table 14. Percentages of 1,097 raptor nest clusters (including Golden Eagles, Ferruginous Hawks, Red-tailed Hawks, and Prairie Falcons) with oil and gas wells within 0.8 and 2.0 km of cluster centroids in 1978 and 2006 in the Rawlins, Wyoming study area.

	Within 0.8 km			Within 2.0 km	
# Wells	1978	2006	# Wells	1978	2006
0	95.1	85.9	0	85.9	73.5
1	3.7	6.6	1	7.1	7.3
2	0.5	2.9	2-5	5.7	8.5
3	0.5	1.7	6-10	0.9	3.8
4	0.2	1.4	11-15	0.3	2.1
5	0.0	0.6	16-20	0.1	2.4
>5	0.0	0.9	>20	0.0	2.5

Table 15. Percentages by land owner/manager of 1,097 raptor nest clusters (including Golden Eagles, Ferruginous Hawks, Red-tailed Hawks, and Prairie Falcons) with no oil and gas wells within 0.8 and 2.0 km of cluster centroids in 1978 and 2006 in the Rawlins, Wyoming study area.

Land Manager	n	Within 0.8 km		Within 2.0 km	
		1978	2006	1978	2006
BLM	609	96	83	86	69
State	68	97	94	84	87
Private	397	94	88	86	78
Other[1]	23	100	96	100	87

[1] Includes Bureau of Reclamation, Water Reserve, and U.S. Forest Service lands.

Objective 2: Describe distributional patterns of nest cluster status in relation to development hotspots.

We identified three energy development hotspots in the Rawlins study area that encompassed at least five raptor nest clusters with ≥5 years of survey history between 1998 and 2006 (Figure 11). Within the three development hotspots, we identified 14 Golden Eagle, 54 Ferruginous Hawk, 1 Red-tailed Hawk, and 2 Prairie Falcon nest clusters that met our initial screening criteria. However, only the Ferruginous Hawk had sufficient representation of nest clusters in both the "used" and "unused" or "active" and "other" categories to support analyses (i.e., at least five nests per year in each category). A comparison of used versus unused and active versus other nest clusters produced nearly identical results (i.e., similar annual trends, group means, and P-values from group mean comparisons), so we report here only the results from the nest-cluster activity analysis. Active clusters ($n = 194$) averaged significantly closer to development-hotspot centers than other clusters ($n = 205$; active mean: -0.38 ± SE of 0.06 standardized units; unused mean: 0.35±0.07 units; $t = 7.94$, $P < 0.001$, df = 396; Figure 12). This may be related to the fact that 46% of the analyzed nest clusters included ANSs installed primarily to mitigate for use of natural-gas condensation tanks by Ferruginous Hawks (sample sizes were not sufficient to exclude clusters containing ANSs).

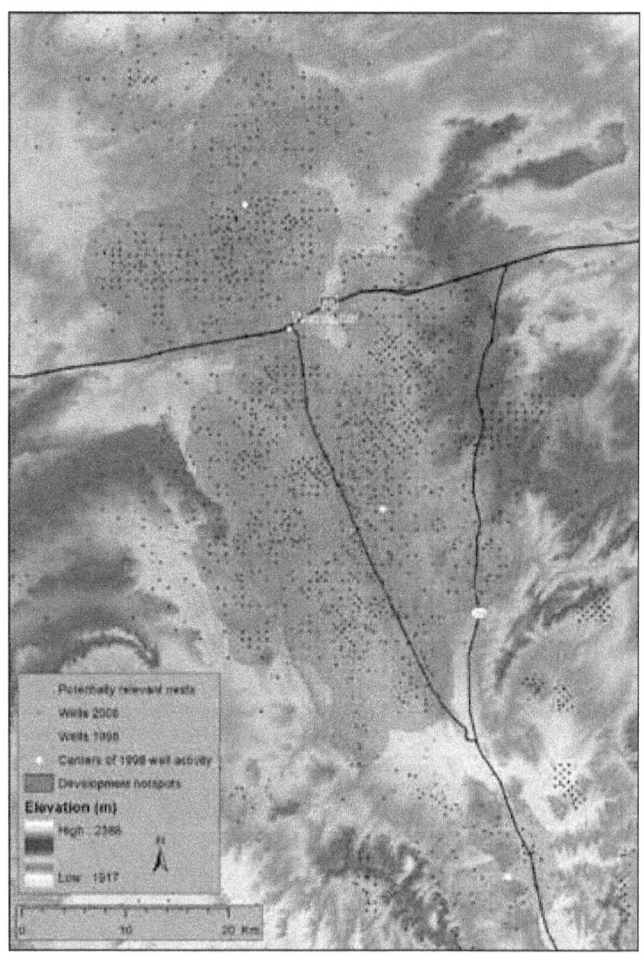

Figure 11. Map depicting the distribution of raptor nests from nest clusters with ≥5 years of survey history between 1998 and 2006 within three oil and gas development "hotspots" in the Rawlins, Wyoming study area.

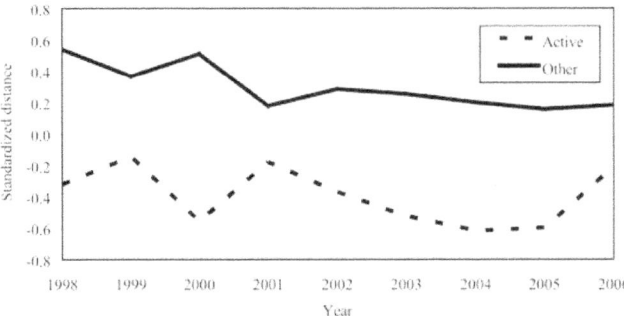

Figure 12. Average standardized distances between development "hotspot" centers and "active" and "other" Ferruginous Hawk nest clusters in the Rawlins, Wyoming study area from 1998 to 2006.

The comparison of pre-1988 and post-1990 kernel densities of active Ferruginous Hawk nests confirmed a distinct distributional shift related to the post-1990 availability of ANSs (Figure 13). Although pockets of relatively limited nesting activity remained in other scattered locations after the ANSs were installed, the highest-density activity centers clearly shifted to locations of ANSs once they were available.

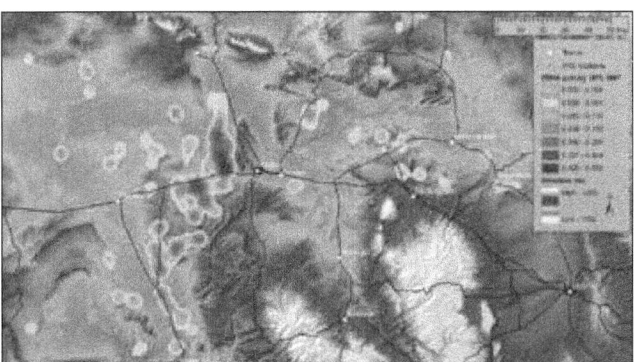

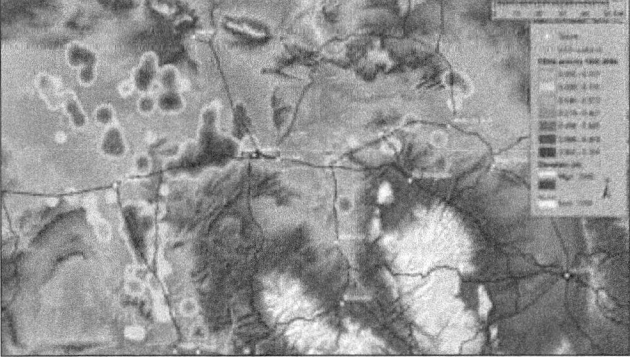

Figure 13. Kernel density (within a 5-km radius) of active Ferruginous Hawk (FEHA) nests in the Rawlins, Wyoming study area relative to 105 artificial nest structure (ANS) locations before (1970–1987, upper panel) and after (1990–2006, lower panel) their installation.

Objective 3: Assess relationships between nest cluster status and development.

a) Describe development patterns near nest clusters.—
The PCAs identified two PCs, or DFs, with eigenvalues >1.0 at both the 0.8 and 2.0-km spatial scales. The two primary PCs were able to explain 56% and 57% of the variation in the 0.8 and 2.0-km scale datasets. The nature of contrasts represented in the primary PCs was similar for both spatial scales (Figure 14) and closely analogous

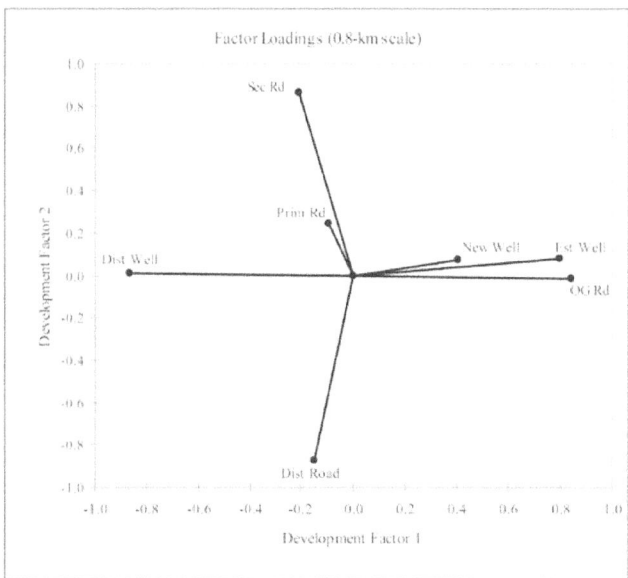

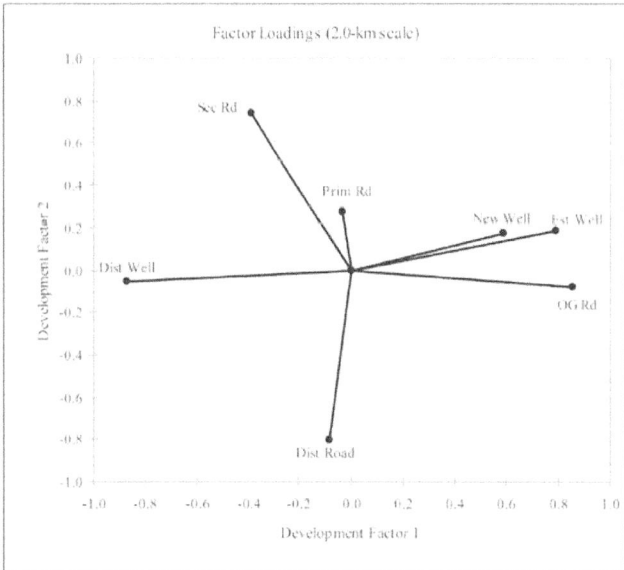

Figure 14. Graphical display of individual development-variable loadings associated with two primary development factors identified by Principal Components Analysis of characteristics associated with 1,097 raptor nest clusters at the 0.8-km and 2.0-km radius spatial scales in the Rawlins, Wyoming study area.

to DF1 and DF2 derived for the Price study area. That is, at both spatial scales, DF1 could be interpreted as representing the overall degree of OG development activity (i.e., increasing total length of OG roads, increasing well density, and decreasing distance to wells), while DF2 could be interpreted as representing the degree of primarily non-OG roads (i.e., increasing total lengths of secondary and primary roads, decreasing distance to roads). Given the straightforward interpretation and high congruence between PCs produced at each scale, we again chose to use DF1 and DF2 scores in place of individual development variables in subsequent analyses.

b) Annual nest-cluster activity.—Initial species-specific analyses of nest-cluster status (with the dependent variable classified as used/unused or active/other) versus DF1 and DF2 (i.e., logistic regression without inclusion of vegetation and climatic variables) revealed significant relationships between development and the annual status of nest clusters. Golden Eagle nest-cluster use and activity were both negatively related to DF1 at both the 0.8-km and 2.0-km spatial scales (i.e., use and activity declined with increasing OG development), and positively related to DF2 at the 2.0-km scale (use and activity increased with non-OG roads at the larger scale). A slightly more complicated scenario emerged for Ferruginous Hawk non-ANS nest clusters. Non-ANS nest-cluster use and activity related negatively to OG development at both spatial scales if only one DF1 variable was included in the model, but with both 0.8 and 2.0-km variables in the model, a positive relationship was indicated at the 2.0-km scale. A similar scenario applied to non-OG roads: positive relationships at both spatial scales with only one DF2 variable included; negative relationship at the 2.0-km scale with both variables modeled together. An initial inspection of relationships between development variables and Ferruginous Hawk ANS cluster use and activity suggested that both related positively to OG development at both scales and non-OG roads at the 2.0-km scale. In contrast, a negative relationship with non-OG roads within 0.8 km was indicated. Note that opposite relationships with development were observed at non-ANS and ANS nest clusters. Red-tailed Hawk nest-cluster use and activity related negatively to OG development at either spatial scale, while cluster activity related positively to non-OG roads at either scale, suggesting patterns similar to those shown for Golden Eagles. In contrast, Prairie Falcon nest-cluster use and activity related negatively to both OG development and non-OG roads at both spatial scales. This suggests a more pervasive negative relationship with development in general, whether OG-related or not. PCA of the proportional coverage of 19 original landcover/vegetation classes within a 2-km radius of

1,110 raptor nest clusters (including Golden Eagles, Ferruginous Hawks, Red-tailed Hawks, and Prairie Falcons) produced six VFs with eigenvalues >1.0, which collectively explained 66% of the variation in the Rawlins dataset (Table 16). VF1 accounted for 21% of the total variance and distinguished clusters dominated by mixes of mountain and Wyoming big sagebrush, grass, mesic shrubs, and deciduous forest from those dominated by mixed desert shrubs. VF2 accounted for another 17% of the total variation and distinguished clusters dominated by mixes of grass, mountain mahogany, riparian and evergreen forest, and agriculture from those dominated by sagebrush mixes. VF3 accounted for another 8% of the variation and distinguished clusters containing relatively high cover of barren land and low cover of Wyoming big sagebrush. VF4 accounted for another 8% of the variation and distinguished clusters with relatively higher cover of basin big sagebrush and juniper. VF5 accounted for another 6% of the variation and distinguished clusters featuring mixes of basin big sagebrush, riparian shrubs, human habitations, and miscellaneous disturbed lands, but little juniper cover. VF6 accounted for another 6% of the variation and distinguished clusters with relatively high evergreen forest cover from those with relatively high cover of Wyoming big sagebrush, human habitations, and agriculture. Again, note that the primary impetus for producing vegetation PCs was to account for the potential confounding influence of vegetation on cluster status and to determine how vegetation modified relationships between status and development; it is not our intention to provide detailed interpretations of cluster status/vegetation relationships.

An initial graphical examination of relationships between the probability of a cluster being active and climatic variables for the Rawlins study area during the period of highest raptor data quality (i.e., 1998–2006) suggested less distinct relationships between individual parameters (Figure 15) than found in the Price study area. Correlation coefficients suggested that the strongest relationships were between winter precipitation (WintPPT) and cluster activity for Golden Eagles (0.70) and Ferruginous Hawks (0.63) during this period. Additionally, a general depression of activity occurred during 2002, the year of severest drought, similar to trends observed in the Price study area. However, over the entire study period (i.e., 1978–2006), all climate/activity correlations were less than 0.33, suggesting generally weak relationships between individual climate variables and cluster activity over this longer time frame.

Adding landcover/vegetation and climatic variables to the models of cluster use and activity revealed additional complexity, with all final best-fitting models including

Table 16. Summary of Principal Components Analysis describing six primary landcover/vegetation factors with eigenvalues >1.0 derived from 19 original landcover/vegetation variables representing proportional coverage within 2 km of 1,109 raptor nest clusters in the Rawlins, Wyoming study area (* indicates high loadings that comprise the primary variables involved in each factor).

Vegetation/landcover variables	Vegetation Factors produced by PCA					
	1	2	3	4	5	6
Grass	-0.054	0.726*	-0.222	-0.309	0.191	0.057
Sagebrush/grass	0.841*	-0.282	-0.083	0.085	-0.051	-0.075
Wyoming big sagebrush	-0.262	-0.478*	0.527*	-0.328	0.010	0.398*
Mountain big sagebrush	0.856*	0.023	0.190	-0.059	0.109	-0.134
Wyoming/mountain big sagebrush	0.762*	-0.425*	-0.021	0.195	0.130	0.018
Basin big sagebrush	-0.078	-0.429*	0.097	0.502*	0.421*	-0.188
Desert shrub	-0.637*	-0.296	-0.399*	0.364	-0.190	-0.190
Mountain mahogany	0.029	0.614*	-0.356	0.049	0.228	0.080
Mesic shrub	0.840*	-0.232	-0.175	-0.152	-0.082	0.085
Riparian shrub	0.034	0.415	-0.252	0.063	0.350	0.296
Riparian forest	0.283	0.727*	0.309	0.164	-0.061	-0.068
Deciduous forest	0.800*	0.034	-0.162	-0.041	-0.075	0.091
Evergreen forest mix	0.167	0.513	0.364	0.047	0.079	-0.568*
Juniper	0.093	0.051	0.307	0.564*	-0.363	0.279
Barren	0.153	-0.021	-0.706*	0.185	-0.231	0.072
Disturbed land	-0.037	-0.094	0.064	0.250	0.470*	-0.019
Water	-0.024	0.323	0.061	0.342	-0.270	-0.115
Agriculture	0.143	0.566*	0.235	0.295	-0.183	0.394*
Human habitation	-0.010	-0.044	0.020	0.313	0.446*	0.308
Cumulative variance explained	21%	38%	46%	54%	60%	66%

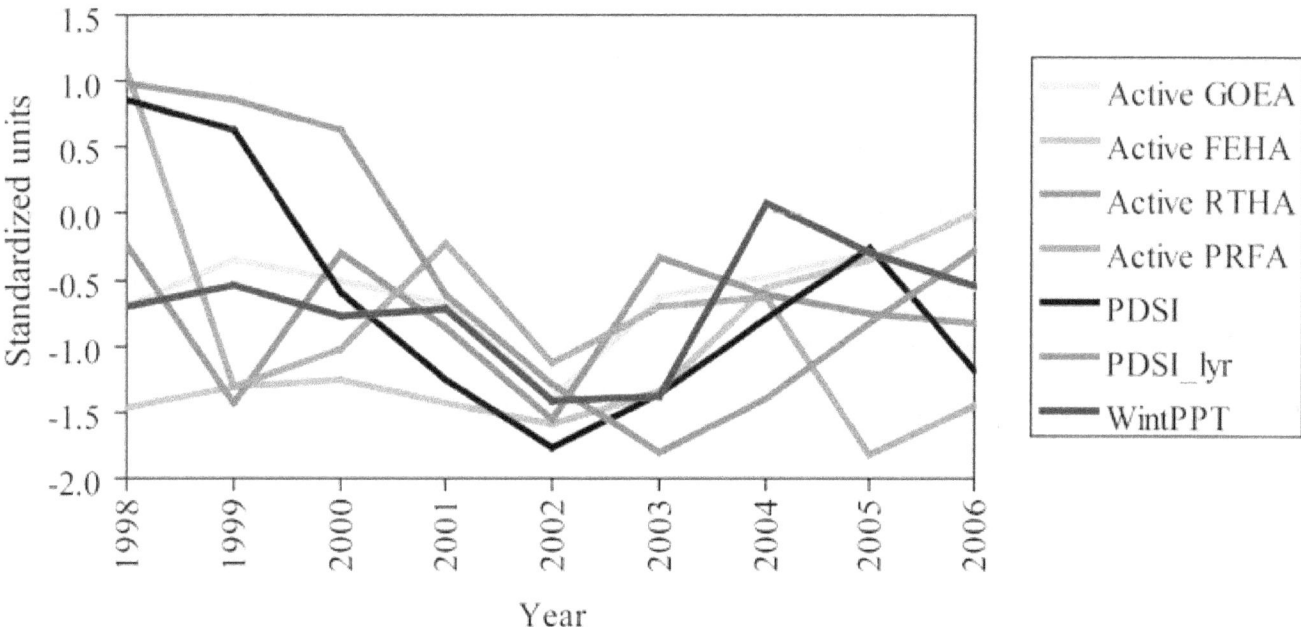

Figure 15. Comparison of annual trends in species-specific proportional nest activity, the Palmer Drought Severity Index (PDSI; higher values = less drought severity), PDSI in the previous year (PDSI_lyr), and winter precipitation (WintPPT) in the Rawlins, Wyoming study area from 1998–2006 (period of greatest raptor data quality). All measures have been standardized using the entire 1978–2006 dataset for direct comparison.

one or more landcover/vegetation factors and, with one exception, one or more annual climatic variables (Tables 17–24).

With the six VFs and climate variables incorporated as potential covariates along with the 4 DFs, we identified four top models that helped differentiate between used (n = 721 events) and unused (n = 592) Golden Eagle clusters (Table 17). Top models reflected only slight variations on a common theme and suggested cluster use related positively to VF1, VF2, PDSI, and WintPPT, and negatively related to PDSI_lyr. No development factors were included in the top models, suggesting that OG or other development patterns did not greatly affect the probability of a Golden Eagle nest cluster being used in a given year. Instead, primarily habitat and especially climatic variation drove patterns of Golden Eagle nest-cluster use. Cluster use apparently increased with cover of grass, mountain mahogany, and agriculture, and declined with Wyoming big sagebrush (VF2); and increased with cover of general sagebrush, mountain and mixed mountain/Wyoming big sagebrush, mesic shrub, and deciduous forest, and declined with cover of desert shrub (VF1). The climate variables suggested that cluster use was greater in wetter years (PDSI) and following wetter winters (WintPPT), particularly when the previous year was drier (PDSI_lyr); in other words, use was greater in "drought recovery" years.

The four top models comparing active (n = 671 events) and other (n = 642) Golden Eagle nest clusters suggested that the probability of a cluster being active related positively to VF2, PDSI, and WintPPT, and negatively related to DF1_2K and PDSI_lyr (Table 18). Thus, increasing OG development with 2.0 km of clusters influenced only actual breeding attempts negatively. Both top use and activity models suggested similar positive relationships to increased cover of grass, mountain mahogany, and agriculture, but declining Wyoming big sagebrush cover (VF2), and positive relationships with drought recovery years (combination of relationships to all three climate variables).

We identified six top models that helped explain differences between used (n = 730 events) and unused (n = 1,539) non-ANS Ferruginous Hawk nest clusters (Table 19). However, even the best model among the top six failed the Hosmer-Lemeshow goodness-of-fit test (X = 17.31, df = 8, P = 0.027; note that a significant result implies a significant mismatch between predicted and actual nest-cluster classifications given the model), indicating that the models provided very little effective discrimination ability. Overall, the top models suggested that cluster use related positively to DF2_0.8K, VF2, VF3, VF4, VF6, PDSI, and WintPPT, and negatively to DF2_2K, VF5, and PDSI_lyr. This suggests that the probability of a Ferruginous Hawk nest cluster being

Table 17. Top multiple logistic regression models (ΔAICc <4.0) describing relationships between the probability of a Golden Eagle nest cluster being "used" in a given year and oil and gas development factors (DFs), landcover/vegetation factors (VFs), and climate variables in the Rawlins, Wyoming study area.

Development Factors	Vegetation Factors	Climate Factors	K	Log(L)	ΔAICc	w_i
None	VF1, VF2	PDSI, PDSI_lyr, WintPPT	6	-862.30	0.00	0.35
None	VF1, VF2	PDSI, PDSI_lyr	5	-863.56	0.49	0.27
None	VF2	PDSI, PDSI_lyr, WintPPT	5	-863.84	1.05	0.21
None	VF2	PDSI, PDSI_lyr	4	-865.15	1.65	0.15

Note: K = number of parameters, including constant and error terms; Log(L) = log likelihood; w_i = Akaike's weight, indicating probability of model given the data (Burnham and Anderson 2002).

Table 18. Top multiple logistic regression models (ΔAICc <4.0) describing relationships between the probability of a Golden Eagle nest cluster being "active" in a given year and oil and gas development factors (DFs), landcover/vegetation factors (VFs), and climate variables in the Rawlins, Wyoming study area.

Development Factors	Vegetation Factors	Climate Factors	K	Log(L)	ΔAICc	w_i
None	VF2	PDSI, PDSI_lyr, WintPPT	6	-851.07	0.00	0.45
None	VF2	PDSI, PDSI_lyr, WintPPT	5	-852.52	0.88	0.29
DF1_2K	VF2	PDSI, PDSI_lyr	5	-853.19	2.22	0.15
None	VF2	PDSI, PDSI_lyr	4	-854.93	3.67	0.07

Note: K = number of parameters, including constant and error terms; Log(L) = log likelihood; w_i = Akaike's weight, indicating probability of model given the data (Burnham and Anderson 2002).

Table 19. Top multiple logistic regression models (ΔAICc <4.0) describing relationships between the probability of a non-ANS Ferruginous Hawk nest cluster being "used" in a given year and oil and gas development factors (DFs), landcover/vegetation factors (VFs), and climate variables in the Rawlins, Wyoming study area.

Development Factors	Vegetation Factors	Climate Factors	Interactions	K	Log(L)	ΔAICc	w_i
DF2_0.8K, DF2_2K	VF2, VF3, VF4, VF5, VF6	PDSI, PDSI_lyr, WintPPT	DF2_0.8K*VF4	12	-1325.67	0.00	0.28
DF_0.8K, DF2_2K	VF2, VF3, VF4, VF6	PDSI, PDSI_lyr, WintPPT	DF2_0.8K*VF4	11	-1326.89	0.42	0.23
DF2_0.8K, DF2_2K	VF2, VF3, VF4, VF6	PDSI, PDSI_lyr, WintPPT	DF2_0.8K*VF6	11	-1327.23	1.08	0.16
DF2_0.8K, DF2_2K	VF2, VF3, VF4, VF6	PDSI_lyr, WintPPT	DF2_0.8K*VF4	10	-1328.80	2.22	0.09
DF2_0.8K, DF2_2K	VF2, VF3, VF4, VF6	PDSI_lyr, WintPPT	DF2_0.8K*VF6	10	-1329.25	3.11	0.06
DF2_0.8K, DF2_2K	VF2, VF3, VF4, VF5, VF6	WintPPT	DF2_0.8K*VF4	10	-1329.58	3.77	0.04

Note: K = number of parameters, including constant and error terms; Log(L) = log likelihood; w_i = Akaike's weight, indicating probability of model given the data (Burnham and Anderson 2002).

used tended to increase as the relative abundance of non-OG roads increased and the proximity of the nearest road decreased within 0.8 km of the cluster centroid, but the strength of those associations diminished with distance. Interactions between DF2_0.8K and VF4 or VF6 also occurred in all top models, suggesting that the positive influence of relatively abundant non-OG roads in proximity to nest clusters was enhanced in habitats featuring relatively high cover of juniper, basin big sagebrush, or evergreen forest mix, and/or relatively low cover of Wyoming big sagebrush or agriculture.

The top six models comparing active ($n = 637$ events) and other ($n = 1,632$) non-ANS Ferruginous Hawk nest clusters were similar to the top use models (Table 20). Again the top-ranking activity model failed the Hosmer–Lemeshow goodness-of-fit test ($X = 37.48$, df = 8, $P < 0.001$). Generally, cluster activity related positively to

Table 20. Top multiple logistic regression models (ΔAICc <4.0) describing the relationships between the probability of a non-ANS Ferruginous Hawk nest cluster being "active" in a given year and various oil and gas development factors (DFs), landcover/vegetation factors (VFs), climatic variables, and interactions in the Rawlins, Wyoming study area.

Development Factors	Vegetation Factors	Climate Factors	Interactions	K	Log(L)	ΔAICc	w_i
DF1_0.8K, DF2_0.8K, DF2_2K	VF2, VF3, VF4, VF5, VF6	WintPPT	DF2_0.8K*VF3	11	-1246.77	0.00	0.22
DF1_0.8K, DF2_0.8K, DF2_2K	VF2, VF3, VF4, VF6	WintPPT	DF2_0.8K*VF6	10	-1247.79	0.02	0.22
DF1_0.8K, DF2_0.8K, DF2_2K	VF2, VF3, VF4, VF6	WintPPT	DF2_0.8K*VF3	10	-1247.90	0.23	0.20
DF1_0.8K, DF2_0.8K, DF2_2K	VF2, VF4, VF6	WintPPT	DF2_0.8K*VF6	9	-1249.38	1.18	0.12
DF2_0.8K, DF2_2K	VF2, VF3, VF4, VF6	WintPPT	DF2_0.8K*VF6	9	-1249.81	2.05	0.08
DF2_0.8K, DF2_2K	VF2, VF3, VF4, VF6	WintPPT	DF2_0.8K*VF3	9	-1249.87	2.16	0.08

Note: K = number of parameters, including constant and error terms; Log(L) = log likelihood; w_i = Akaike's weight, indicating probability of model given the data (Burnham and Anderson 2002).

DF2_0.8K, VF2, VF3, VF4, VF6, and WintPPT, and negatively to DF1_0.8K, DF2_2K, and VF5, and all top models included a negative interaction between DF2_0.8K and VF6 or VF3. Similar to cluster use, cluster activity related positively to proximate (within 0.8 km) non-OG roads, but this relationship diminished or reversed at the broader spatial scale (2.0 km).

The activity models differed from the use models in suggesting a negative relationship with OG development at the 0.8-km scale, and in not including relationships with PDSI and PDSI_lyr. This suggests that the probability of an actual breeding attempt occurring was more sensitive to changes in OG development levels within 0.8 km of the cluster, but less sensitive to drought conditions than the probability of simple cluster use. The interactions suggested that the positive effect of DF2_0.8K again was enhanced in habitats featuring more evergreen forest and less Wyoming big sagebrush or agriculture (VF6), and was enhanced in habitats with relatively high cover of barren land and low cover of Wyoming big sagebrush and desert shrubs (VF3). We identified four top models that helped explain differences between used ($n = 522$ events) and unused ($n = 935$) Ferruginous Hawk ANS nest clusters (Table 21). As with the top models of non-ANS cluster use and activity, the best model of ANS cluster use failed the Hosmer-Lemeshow goodness-of-fit test ($X = 19.03$, df = 8, $P = 0.015$), suggesting poor model performance. In general, these models suggested that ANS cluster use related positively to DF1_0.8K, DF2_2K, VF2, VF6, and WintPPT, and negatively to DF2_0.8K, VF5, and PDSI, and interactions between DF1_0.8K and VF2 or VF6 were common. The development results suggest that cluster use was highest in areas with relatively high OG

development and correspondingly low density of non-OG roads proximate to nests (0.8-km scale; as expected given the close association of ANSs and OG infrastructure), but relatively high cover of non-OG roads at the larger 2.0-km spatial scale. Again, note that these development relationships at ANS clusters were opposite those detected at non-ANS clusters. ANS cluster use also was greater in areas with increased cover of riparian forest, grass, mountain mahogany, and/or agriculture, but less evergreen forest, disturbed land, human habitation, and/or basin big sagebrush. The variable interactions indicated that the positive effects of proximate OG development were enhanced in habitats featuring relatively high cover of riparian forest, grass, mountain mahogany, agriculture, and/or areas with less evergreen forest mix (all relatively rare components around Ferruginous Hawk ANS nest clusters). Also note that the positive association with winter precipitation is the same as in the non-ANS models, but that the negative association with PDSI (i.e., suggesting that cluster use was greater in drier years) is opposite the relationship seen in the non-ANS models.

We identified three top models from the comparison of active ($n = 596$) versus other ($n = 861$) Ferruginous Hawk ANS nest clusters (Table 22). The top models suggested similar relationships as the use models; however, the best activity model did not fail the goodness-of-fit test. As with use, ANS cluster activity related positively to DF1_0.8K, DF2_2K, VF2, VF6, and WintPPT, negatively to DF2_0.8K, VF5, and PDSI, and an interaction between DF1_0.8K and VF2 was included in all top models. This suggests that both ANS cluster use and activity were highest in areas with relatively high OG development and low non-OG roads proximate to nests (0.8-km scale), but relatively high cover of non-OG roads at the larger

Table 21. Top multiple logistic regression models (ΔAICc <4.0) describing relationships between the probability of a Ferruginous Hawk ANS nest cluster being "used" in a given year and oil and gas development factors (DFs), landcover/vegetation factors (VFs), and climate variables in the Rawlins, Wyoming study area.

Development Factors	Vegetation Factors	Climate Factors	Interactions	K	Log(L)	ΔAICc	w_i
DF1_0.8K, DF2_0.8K, DF2_2K	VF2, VF5, VF6	PDSI, WintPPT	DF1_0.8K*VF2, DF1_0.8K*VF6	11	-908.52	0.00	0.50
DF1_0.8K, DF2_0.8K, DF2_2K	VF2, VF5, VF6	PDSI, WintPPT	DF1_0.8K*VF2, DF1_0.8K*VF5	11	-909.52	1.99	0.18
DF1_0.8K	VF2, VF5, VF6	PDSI, WintPPT	DF1_0.8K*VF2, DF1_0.8K*VF6	9	-911.78	2.45	0.15
DF1_0.8K	VF2, VF6	PDSI, WintPPT	DF1_0.8K*VF2, DF1_0.8K*VF6	8	-913.05	2.96	0.11

Note: K = number of parameters, including constant and error terms; Log(L) = log likelihood; w_i = Akaike's weight, indicating probability of model given the data (Burnham and Anderson 2002).

Table 22. Top multiple logistic regression models (ΔAICc <4.0) describing the relationships between the probability of a Ferruginous Hawk ANS nest cluster being "active" in a given year and various oil and gas development factors (DFs), landcover/vegetation factors (VFs), climatic variables, and interactions and in the Rawlins, Wyoming study area.

Development Factors	Vegetation Factors	Climate Factors	Interactions	K	Log(L)	ΔAICc	w_i
DF1_0.8K, DF2_0.8K, DF2_2K	VF2, VF5, VF6	PDSI, WintPPT	DF1_0.8K*VF2, DF1_0.8K*VF5	11	-946.14	0.00	0.47
DF1_0.8K, DF2_0.8K, DF2_2K	VF2, VF5, VF6	PDSI, WintPPT	DF1_0.8K*VF2, DF1_0.8K*VF6	11	-947.03	1.79	0.19
DF1_0.8K	VF2, VF5, VF6	PDSI, WintPPT	DF1_0.8K*VF2, DF1_0.8K*VF5, DF1_0.8K*PDSI	10	-948.60	2.88	0.11

Note: K = number of parameters, including constant and error terms; Log(L) = log likelihood; w_i = Akaike's weight, indicating probability of model given the data (Burnham and Anderson 2002).

2.0-km spatial scale. Both cluster use and activity also were greater in areas with increased cover of riparian forest, grass, mountain mahogany, and/or agriculture, but less evergreen forest, disturbed land, human habitation, and/or basin big sagebrush. The consistent interaction in all top use and activity models suggests the positive effects of proximate OG development were enhanced in habitats featuring relatively high cover of riparian forest, grass, mountain mahogany, and/or agriculture. Cluster use and activity were both positively associated with pre-nesting season winter precipitation, but negatively related to overall wetter conditions during the year (PDSI).

We identified 14 top models that helped explain differences between used (*n* = 384 events) and unused (*n* = 200) Red-tailed Hawk nest clusters (Table 23). The top models generally suggested that cluster use related positively to DF1_2K, VF1, VF2, VF3, VF4, and PDSI, and negatively to DF1_0.8K and DF2_2K. A few models also suggested that use related positively to VF6 and

Table 23. Top multiple logistic regression models (ΔAICc <4.0) describing the relationships between the probability of a Red-tailed Hawk nest cluster being "used" in a given year and various oil and gas development factors (DFs), landcover/vegetation factors (VFs), climatic variables, and interactions in the Rawlins, Wyoming study area.

Development Factors	Vegetation Factors	Climate Factors	Interactions	K	Log(L)	ΔAICc	w_i
DF1_0.8K, DF1_2K	VF1, VF2, VF3, VF4	PDSI	DF1_2K*VF2	9	-313.21	0.00	0.20
DF2_2K	VF1, VF2, VF3, VF4	PDSI	DF2_2K*VF1	8	-315.13	1.79	0.08
DF1_0.8K, DF1_2K	VF1, VF3, VF5	PDSI	DF1_2K*VF2	9	-314.33	2.26	0.06
DF2_2K	VF1, VF2, VF3, VF4	PDSI	None	7	-316.71	2.88	0.05
DF1_0.8K, DF1_2K	VF1, VF2, VF3, VF5	PDSI	DF1_2K*VF2	9	-314.67	2.92	0.05
DF1_0.8K, DF1_2K, DF2_2K	VF1, VF2, VF3, VF4	PDSI	None	9	-314.95	3.49	0.04
DF1_0.8K, DF1_2K	VF1, VF2	PDSI	DF1_0.8K*PDSI, DF1_2K*VF2	8	-316.01	3.55	0.03
DF2_2K	VF1, VF2, VF4, VF6	PDSI	None	7	-317.07	3.60	0.03
None	VF1, VF2, VF3, VF5	PDSI	None	6	-318.10	3.60	0.03
DF1_0.8K, DF1_2K	VF1, VF2, VF4, VF6	PDSI	DF1_2K*VF2	9	-315.03	3.64	0.03
DF1_0.8K, DF1_2K	VF1, VF2, VF3, VF4	PDSI	None	8	-316.14	3.80	0.03
DF1_0.8K, DF1_2K	VF1, VF2, VF3, VF5	PDSI	None	8	-316.15	3.82	0.03
None	VF1, VF2, VF3, VF5	PDSI, WintPPT	None	7	-317.22	3.89	0.03
DF2_2K	VF1, VF2	PDSI	DF2_2K*VF1	6	-318.26	3.92	0.03

Note: K = number of parameters, including constant and error terms; Log(L) = log likelihood; w_i = Akaike's weight, indicating probability of model given the data (Burnham and Anderson 2002).

WintPPT and negatively to VF5, while an interaction between DF1_2K and VF2 was present in 5 of the 14 top models. Overall, the models suggested a mixed relationship with OG development, with a negative effect at the smaller 0.8-km scale but a positive effect at the larger 2.0-km spatial scale. Note that this is the opposite pattern shown for Red-tailed Hawks in the Price study area. The significant interaction with VF2 suggested that the apparent positive effect of increasing development at the 2.0-km scale was enhanced in habitats with relatively high cover of riparian forest, grass, mountain mahogany, and/or agriculture, but was diminished in habitats with high cover of Wyoming big sagebrush. Finally, as with most other species and situations, Red-tailed Hawks appeared to benefit from reduced drought severity (PDSI; i.e., wetter conditions) and their nesting activity also varied across habitats.

In contrast to the large number of top Red-tailed Hawk use models, and similar to the case in the Price study area, relatively few (four) top models were selected to distinguish between active ($n = 359$ events) and other ($n = 225$) Red-tailed Hawk nest clusters in the Rawlins study area (Table 24). In contrast to the Red-tailed Hawk use models, no DFs were included in the top activity models. Otherwise, both the use and activity models suggested similar positive relationships with VF1, VF2, VF4, VF6, PDSI, and WintPPT. These results suggest that the probability of an actual breeding attempt occurring in a Red-tailed Hawk nest cluster was largely independent of OG development activity, but did vary significantly across certain habitat types and in relation to drought severity. Increased cluster use and activity apparently occurred in wetter years and, to a lesser extent, following wetter pre-nesting season winters (WintPPT).

We identified 10 top models that helped differentiate between used ($n = 307$ events) and unused ($n = 148$) Prairie Falcon nest clusters (Table 25). The top models indicated that use related positively to VF1, VF2, VF3,

Table 24. Top multiple logistic regression models (ΔAICc <4.0) describing relationships between the probability of a Red-tailed Hawk cluster being "active" in a given year and oil and gas development factors (DFs), landcover/vegetation factors (VFs), and climatic variables in the Rawlins, Wyoming study area.

Development Factors	Vegetation Factors	Climate Factors	K	Log(L)	ΔAICc	w_i
None	VF1, VF2, VF4, VF6	PDSI	6	-321.89	0.00	0.39
None	VF1, VF2, VF4, VF6	PDSI, WintPPT	7	-321.21	0.69	0.28
None	VF1, VF2	PDSI	4	-324.58	1.28	0.21
None	VF1, VF2, VF4, VF6	PDSI_1yr, WintPPT	7	-322.75	3.76	0.06

Note: K = number of parameters, including constant and error terms; Log(L) = log likelihood; w_i = Akaike's weight, indicating probability of model given the data (Burnham and Anderson 2002).

Table 25. Top multiple logistic regression models (ΔAICc <4.0) describing relationships between the probability of a Prairie Falcon cluster being "used" in a given year and oil and gas development factors (DFs), landcover/vegetation factors (VFs), and climate variables in the Rawlins, Wyoming study area.

Development Factors	Vegetation Factors	Climate Factors	Interactions	K	Log(L)	ΔAICc	w_i
DF1_0.8K	VF1, VF2, VF3, VF5	WintPPT	DF1_0.8K*VF3	8	-264.52	0.00	0.19
DF1_0.8K, DF2_0.8K	VF1, VF5	WintPPT	DF2_0.8K*VF1	8	-265.27	1.50	0.09
DF1_0.8K, DF2_0.8K	VF1, VF5	WintPPT	DF2_0.8K*VF1	7	-266.35	1.58	0.09
DF1_0.8K	VF1, VF2, VF3, VF5	PDSI, PDSI_1yr	DF1_0.8K*VF3	9	-264.49	2.03	0.07
DF1_0.8K	VF1, VF2, VF3, VF5	WintPPT	None	7	-266.70	2.28	0.06
DF2_0.8K	VF1	PDSI, WintPPT	DF2_0.8K*VF1	6	-267.83	2.46	0.06
DF1_0.8K	VF1, VF2, VF3, VF5	PDSI	DF1_0.8K*VF3	8	-265.89	2.73	0.05
DF2_0.8K	VF1	WintPPT	DF2_0.8K*VF1	5	-269.02	2.79	0.05
None	VF1, VF2, VF3, VF5	WintPPT	None	6	-268.02	2.84	0.05
DF1_0.8K, DF2_0.8K	VF1	WintPPT	D2_0.8K*VF1	6	-268.31	3.42	0.04

Note: K = number of parameters, including constant and error terms; Log(L) = log likelihood; w_i = Akaike's weight, indicating probability of model given the data (Burnham and Anderson 2002).

PDSI, and WintPPT, and negatively to DF1_0.8K, DF2_0.8K, VF5, and PDSI_lyr. These results suggest that the probability of a Prairie Falcon nest cluster being used declined as OG development increased and in areas where the prevalence of non-OG roads was high within 0.8 km. Further, interactions between DF1_0.8K and VF3 and between DF2_0.8K and VF1 were present in three and five of the top models, respectively. The first interaction suggests that the negative influence of OG development within 0.8-km of clusters was enhanced in habitats featuring relatively high cover of barren land, but diminished in habitats with relatively high cover of Wyoming big sagebrush. The second interaction suggests that the negative influence of non-OG roads within 0.8-km of clusters was enhanced in habitats featuring mixes of mountain and Wyoming big sagebrush, mesic shrubs, and deciduous forest, and diminished or reversed in habitats dominated by mixed desert shrubs. Winter precipitation was in every model, indicating use was positively associated with wetter winters prior to the nesting season.

We identified four top models that helped distinguish between active (n = 279 events) and other (n = 176) Prairie Falcon nest clusters (Table 26). These models indicated that the probability of a cluster being active related positively to VF1, VF2, VF3, PDSI, and WintPPT, and negatively to DF1_2K, DF2_2K, VF5, and PDSI_lyr. These results were similar to those derived from the use models, except that the activity models suggested relationships with development factors were best modeled at the 2.0-km scale, rather than the 0.8-km scale. The activity models also identified a similar interaction between DF1 (but at the 2.0-km scale) and VF3. Again, this suggests that the negative influence of OG development was enhanced in habitats featuring relatively high cover of barren land, but diminished in habitats with relatively high cover of Wyoming big sagebrush. Cluster

activity was also consistently and positively associated with reduced drought severity.

c) Proportional nest-cluster activity.—We identified 151 non-ANS Ferruginous Hawk, 42 Golden Eagle, 17 Red-tailed Hawk, and 9 Prairie Falcon nest clusters with at least five years of survey history between 1998 and 2006. Sample-size limitations precluded investigation of proportional nest-cluster use and activity for Red-tailed Hawks and Prairie Falcons.

The top eight proportional-use models for Golden Eagles performed relatively well, with the best model accounting for 43.8% (adjusted R^2 value) of the variance in proportional use. Overall, the top models suggested that proportional cluster use related positively to DF1_0.8K or DF1_2K, DF2_2K, and VarDF2_0.8K, and negatively to VarDF1_2K or VarDF1_0.8K (only one top model), VF1, VF3, VF4, and VF6 (Table 27). These results suggest that the proportion of years in which Golden Eagle clusters were used increased in areas with relatively high OG development, but low variance in OG development levels at the broader 2.0-km spatial scale, and a relatively high prevalence of non-OG roads and high variance in the representation of non-OG roads within 0.8 km. The variance detected in non-OG roads could be driven only by shifting nest use within a cluster across years, because non-OG road representation in the landscape was static. As a result, the positive association between proportional use and VarDF2_0.8K must reflect greater use of clusters with more variable non-OG conditions across alternate nests. We also detected this relationship for Golden Eagles in the Price area.

The top 11 activity models for Golden Eagles also appeared to perform well, with the best model accounting for 53.5% of the variance in proportional

Table 26. Top multiple logistic regression models (ΔAICc <4.0) describing relationships between the probability of a Prairie Falcon cluster being "active" in a given year and oil and gas development factors (DFs), landcover/vegetation factors (VFs), and climate variables in the Rawlins, Wyoming study area.

Development Factors	Vegetation Factors	Climate Factors	Interactions	K	Log(L)	ΔAICc	w_i
DF1_2K, DF2_2K	VF1, VF2, VF3, VF5	PDSI, WintPPT	DF1_2K*VF3	10	-256.50	0.00	0.36
DF1_2K	VF1, VF2, VF3, VF5	PDSI, WintPPT	DF1_2K*VF3	9	-257.70	0.32	0.31
DF1_2K	VF1, VF2, VF3, VF5	PDSI, PDSI_lyr	DF1_2K*VF3	9	-258.20	1.32	0.19
DF1_2K	VF1, VF2, VF3, VF5	PDSI	DF1_2K*VF3	8	-259.61	2.03	0.13

Note: K = number of parameters, including constant and error terms; Log(L) = log likelihood; w_i = Akaike's weight, indicating probability of model given the data (Burnham and Anderson 2002).

Table 27. Top multiple regression models (ΔAICc <4.0) describing relationships between proportional "use" of Golden Eagle nest clusters (i.e., proportion of years in which evidence of nest tending or breeding was obtained) and oil and gas development factors (DFs; cluster averages and variances) and average landcover/vegetation factors (VFs) in the Rawlins, Wyoming study area.

Development Factors	Vegetation Factors	K	RSS	ΔAICc	w_i
DF1_0.8K, DF2_2K, VarDF1_0.8K, VarDF2_0.8K	VF3, VF4	7	1.27	0.00	0.22
DF1_0.8K, DF2_2K, VarDF2_0.8K, VarDF1_2K	VF3, VF4, VF6	8	1.19	0.49	0.17
DF1_0.8K, DF2_2K, VarDF2_0.8K, VarDF1_2K	VF1, VF4, VF6	8	1.21	1.15	0.12
DF1_2K, DF2_2K, VarDF2_0.8K, VarDF1_2K	VF1, VF4, VF6	8	1.24	2.29	0.07
DF1_2K, DF2_2K, VarDF2_0.8K, VarDF1_2K	VF3, VF4	7	1.34	2.29	0.07
DF1_2K, DF2_2K, VarDF2_0.8K, VarDF1_2K	VF3, VF4, VF6	8	1.25	2.56	0.06
DF1_0.8K, DF2_2K, VarDF2_0.8K, VarDF1_2K	VF2	6	1.45	2.60	0.06
DF1_2K, DF2_2K, VarDF2_0.8K, VarDF1_2K	VF2	6	1.46	2.86	0.053

Note: Top model total R^2 = 55.8%, adjusted R^2 = 43.8%. K = number of parameters, including constant and error terms; RSS = residual sum of squares; w_i = Akaike's weight, indicating probability of model given the data (Burnham and Anderson 2002).

activity. The top models suggested that the proportion of years in which clusters supported a breeding attempt related positively to DF1_0.8K or DF1_2K, DF2_2K, VarDF2_0.8K or VarDF2_2K, and VF2, and negatively to VarDF1_2K, VF1, VF3, VF4, and VF6 (Table 28). The relationships between proportional activity or use and OG development were overall very similar, suggesting that proportional use and activity were higher in areas

with more but less variable OG development, and in areas with both more and more variable non-OG road networks.

The best model of proportional use at non-ANS Ferruginous Hawk nest clusters explained 37.8% of the variance in use. Overall, the top seven proportional-use models revealed positive relationships with DF1_2K,

Table 28. Top multiple regression models (ΔAICc <4.0) describing relationships between proportional "activity" of Golden Eagle nest clusters (i.e., proportion of years in which a breeding attempt was confirmed) and oil and gas development factors (DFs; cluster averages and variances) and average landcover/vegetation factors (VFs) in the Rawlins, Wyoming study area.

Development Factors	Vegetation Factors	K	RSS	ΔAICc	w_i
DF1_0.8K, DF2_2K, VarDF2_0.8K, VarDF1_2K	VF2, VF4, VF6	8	0.83	0.00	0.18
DF1_0.8K, DF2_2K, VarDF1_2K, VarDF2_2K	VF2	6	0.99	0.71	0.12
DF1_0.8K, DF2_2K, VarDF2_0.8K, VarDF1_2K	VF3, VF4, VF6	8	0.87	1.58	0.08
DF1_2K, DF2_2K, VarDF2_0.8K, VarDF1_2K	VF2, VF4, VF6	8	0.87	1.63	0.08
DF1_0.8K, DF2_2K, VarDF2_0.8K, VarDF1_2K	VF4, VF6	7	0.95	2.13	0.06
DF1_0.8K, DF2_2K, VarDF2_0.8K, VarDF1_2K	VF2	6	1.03	2.42	0.05
DF1_0.8K, DF2_2K, VarDF2_0.8K, VarDF1_2K	VF1, VF4, VF6	8	0.88	2.45	0.05
DF1_2K, DF2_2K, VarDF2_0.8K, VarDF1_2K	VF2	6	1.05	3.35	0.03
DF2_2K, VarDF2_0.8K	VF2, VF4, VF6	6	1.06	3.59	0.03
DF1_2K, DF2_2K, VarDF2_0.8K, VarDF1_2K	VF4, VF6	7	0.99	3.78	0.03
DF1_0.8K, DF2_2K, VarDF2_0.8K	VF2, VF4, VF6	7	0.99	3.82	0.03

Note: Top model total R^2 = 61.4%, adjusted R^2 = 53.5%. K = number of parameters, including constant and error terms; RSS = residual sum of squares; w_i = Akaike's weight indicating probability of model given the data (Burnham and Anderson 2002).

DF2_0.8K, VarDF2_0.8K, and all vegetation factors (but not simultaneously), and a negative relationship with DF1_0.8K (Table 29). These results suggest that proportional use of non-ANS nest clusters was highest in areas with relatively low OG development and high variance in non-OG roads at within 0.8 km, and that the negative relationship with OG development diminished or reversed at the 2.0 km scale. As with both Price and Rawlins Golden Eagles, the association between Ferruginous Hawk proportional cluster use and variance in non-OG roads likely reflects greater use of clusters with more variable non-OG conditions at alternate nests. All top models also revealed positive relationships with VF2, VF4, and VF6.

The best model of proportional activity at non-ANS Ferruginous Hawk nest clusters had a similar explanatory ability as the best use model, accounting for 35.4% of the variance in proportional activity. The top five proportional activity models indicated positive

relationships with DF1_2K, DF2_0.8K, VarDF2_0.8K, and all vegetation factors (but not simultaneously), and a negative relationship with DF1_0.8K (Table 30). These results suggest similar relationships for both proportional activity and use of non-ANS nest clusters in relation to OG development. All use and activity models also revealed positive relationships with VF2. This suggests that use and activity were greater at clusters with relatively high cover of riparian forest, grass, mountain mahogany, and/or agriculture.

Objective 4: Assess Ferruginous Hawk nest success and productivity in relation to development.

It was our intention to investigate differences in nest success and productivity at a subset of Ferruginous Hawk nest clusters in relation to development factors as well as nest substrate (including ANSs) and accessibility.

Table 29. Top multiple regression models (ΔAICc <4.0) describing relationships between proportional use of non-ANS Ferruginous Hawk nest clusters (i.e., proportion of years in which evidence of nest tending or breeding was obtained) and various oil and gas development factors (DFs) and landcover/vegetation factors (VFs) in the Rawlins, Wyoming study area.

Development Factors	Vegetation Factors	K	RSS	ΔAICc	w_i
DF1_0.8K, DF2_0.8K, DF1_2K, VarDF2_0.8K	VF2, VF4, VF5, VF6	9	4.85	0.00	0.20
DF1_0.8K, DF1_2K, VarDF2_0.8K	VF2, VF4, VF5, VF6	8	4.93	0.22	0.18
DF1_2K, VarDF2_0.8K	VF2, VF4, VF5, VF6	7	5.02	0.64	0.14
DF1_0.8K, DF1_2K, VarDF2_0.8K	VF2, VF3, VF4, VF6	8	4.96	1.22	0.11
DF1_0.8K, DF2_0.8K, DF1_2K, VarDF2_0.8K	VF2, VF3, VF4, VF6	9	4.89	1.23	0.11
DF1_2K, VarDF2_0.8K	VF2, VF3, VF4, VF6	7	5.06	2.01	0.07
DF1_0.8K, DF2_0.8K, DF1_2K, VarDF2_0.8K	VF1, VF2, VF4, VF6	9	4.97	3.73	0.03

Note: Top model total R^2 = 41.2%, adjusted R^2 = 37.8%. K = number of parameters, including constant and error terms; RSS = residual sum of squares; w_i = Akaike's weight, indicating probability of model given the data (Burnham and Anderson 2002).

Table 30. Top multiple regression models (ΔAICc <4.0) describing relationships between proportional activity of non-ANS Ferruginous Hawk nest clusters (i.e., proportion of years in which a breeding attempt was confirmed) and various oil and gas development factors (DFs) and landcover/vegetation factors (VFs) in the Rawlins, Wyoming study area.

Development Factors	Vegetation Factors	K	RSS	ΔAICc	w_i
DF1_0.8K, DF2_0.8K, DF1_2K, VarDF2_0.8K	VF2, VF4, VF5, VF6	9	4.47	0.00	0.35
DF1_0.8K, DF2_0.8K, DF1_2K, VarDF2_0.8K	VF1, VF2, VF4, VF6	9	4.53	2.07	0.12
DF1_0.8K, DF1_2K, VarDF2_0.8K	VF2, VF4, VF5, VF6	8	4.62	2.79	0.09
DF1_0.8K , DF2_0.8K, DF1_2K, VarDF2_0.8K	VF2	6	4.79	3.49	0.06
DF1_0.8K, DF2_0.8K, DF1_2K, VarDF2_0.8K	VF2, VF3, VF4, VF6	9	4.59	3.88	0.05

Note: Top model total R^2 = 38.9%, adjusted R^2 = 35.4%. K = number of parameters, including constant and error terms; RSS = residual sum of squares; w_i = Akaike's weight, indicating probability of model given the data (Burnham and Anderson 2002).

Inspection of breeding-event classifications by success and productivity groupings indicated unacceptably inequitable sample sizes across the original 10 substrate and four collapsed substrate/accessibility categories, but an acceptable array when collapsed to just two categories: accessible and inaccessible (Tables 31 and 32). After additional inspection of breeding-event cross-classifications, we chose to limit our assessment of success and productivity to these two categories. Of 283 breeding events ultimately classified as accessible, 84% were on natural substrates and none was on an ANSs. Of 951 breeding events classified as inaccessible, 87% were located on manmade substrates, with 79% on ANSs.

We first compared successful ($n = 177$) and failed ($n = 106$) accessible nests, but identified only nine significant models (Table 33) and the best model failed the Homer-Lemeshow goodness-of-fit test ($X = 19.862$, df = 8, $P = 0.011$). Although the poor fit prohibits strict interpretation, for consistency we outline the general relationships suggested by the models. Development factors did not enter any top models, but variation across certain habitat types and in relation to PDSI was evident. Nest success at accessible nests related positively to VF2, VF5, and PDSI, and negatively related to VF4 and VF6.

Similar to nest success, a comparison of productivity at accessible nests ($n = 283$) produced only nine significant

Table 31. Summary of confirmed Ferruginous Hawk breeding events in the Rawlins, Wyoming study area between 1976–2006 classified by nest substrate and the number of nestlings raised to ≥80% of average fledging age.

Nest Substrate[1]	Number of nestlings produced						
	0	1	2	3	4	5	Total
ANS	53	54	160	307	162	14	750
CLF	4	6	5	8	5	1	29
DCT		2	2	8	2		14
EGT	2	3	9	12	5	1	32
ERR	6	2	4	8	6		26
GHS	25	3	6	6	3	1	44
MMS	8	5	20	34	21		88
NGS	7	1	7	12	4		31
SHB	3		1	6	2		12
ROF	59	10	42	60	30	7	208
Total	167	86	256	461	240	24	1234

[1] ANS = artificial nest structure; CLF = cliff; DCT = deciduous tree; EGT = evergreen tree; ERR = erosional feature; GHS = ground/hillside; MMS = other manmade structure; NGS = natural gas structure; SHB = shrub; ROF = other rock feature.

Table 32. Summary of confirmed Ferruginous Hawk breeding events in the Rawlins, Wyoming study area between 1976–2006 classified by nest substrate/accessibility categories and the number of nestlings produced to ≥80% of average fledging age.

Substrate / Accessibility Category[1]	Number of nestlings produced						
	0	1	2	3	4	5	Total
MM-ACC	9	2	14	15	5	0	45
NAT-ACC	97	16	51	55	17	2	238
Total accessible	106	18	65	70	22	2	283
MM-INACC	59	58	173	338	182	14	824
NAT-INACC	2	10	18	53	36	8	127
Total inaccessible	61	68	191	391	218	22	951
Grand Total	167	86	256	461	240	24	1234

[1] MM-ACC = manmade accessible; MM-INACC = manmade inaccessible; NAT-ACC = natural accessible; NAT-INACC = natural inaccessible.

Table 33. All significant multiple logistic regression models describing relationships between nesting success of accessible Ferruginous Hawk nests in a given year and oil and gas development factors (DFs), landcover/vegetation factors (VFs), and climate variables in the Rawlins, Wyoming study area. Top models are those with ΔAICc values <4.0.

Development Factors	Vegetation Factors	Climate Variables	K	Log(L)	ΔAICc	w$_i$
None	VF2	PDSI	3	-182.86	0.00	0.32
None	VF2	None	2	-184.66	1.54	0.15
None	VF3, VF4	PDSI	4	-182.70	1.76	0.13
None	VF4, VF6	PDSI	4	-182.86	2.07	0.11
None	VF3, VF5	PDSI	4	-183.21	2.78	0.08
None	None	PDSI	2	-185.49	3.19	0.06
None	VF3, VF4	None	3	-184.53	3.33	0.06
None	V4, VF6	None	3	-184.67	3.62	0.05
None	VF3, VF5	None	3	-185.09	4.46	0.03

Note: K = number of parameters, including constant and error terms; Log(L) = log likelihood; w$_i$ = Akaike's weight, indicating probability of model given the data (Burnham and Anderson 2002).

models (Table 34) and the best model explained little of the variance (adjusted R^2 = 3.2%). Ignoring their obvious weakness, the models appeared to suggest that productivity at accessible nests related positively to DF1_0.8K, VF2, and PDSI, and negatively related to VF4 and VF6. Thus, productivity but not nesting success appeared to show a weak positive influence of increasing OG development activity within 0.8 km of nest clusters. Otherwise, both nest success and productivity varied across certain habitat types and benefited from decreasing drought severity.

A comparison of nest successes (*n* = 890) and failures (*n* = 61) at inaccessible nests produced 20 top models with considerable variation (Table 35). As found at accessible

nests, the top model of nest success at inaccessible nests failed the Hosmer-Lemeshow goodness-of-fit test (X = 15.653, df = 8, P = 0.048). Again, for the sake of consistency, we summarize the apparent trends despite the poor model fit. In general, nest success at inaccessible nest related positively to DF1 (at either spatial scale) and negatively to VF3, VF4, or VF6, and PDSI or WintPPT. Fewer models suggested that nest success related positively to VF2 or negatively to DF2_0.8K. Thus, these models suggested a general positive association with increasing OG development and the same negative relationship with drought severity (i.e., higher success with increasing drought severity) as indicated in previous ANS-only models. In this case, however, a negative relationship with winter precipitation often substituted for

Table 34. All significant multiple linear regression models describing relationships between productivity per nest start at accessible Ferruginous Hawk nests and oil and gas development factors (DFs), landcover/vegetation factors (VFs), and climate variables in the Rawlins, Wyoming study area. Top models are those with ΔAICc values <4.0.

Development Factors	Vegetation Factors	Climate Variables	K	RSS	ΔAICc	w$_i$
DF1_0.8K	VF2	PDSI	4	550.82	0.00	0.31
None	VF2	PDSI	3	555.82	0.49	0.24
None	None	PDSI	2	561.32	1.21	0.17
DF1_0.8K	VF4, VF6	PDSI	5	550.36	1.85	0.12
None	VF4, VF6	PDSI	4	555.14	2.21	0.10
DF1_0.8K	VF2	None	3	565.89	5.56	0.02
None	VF2	None	2	570.25	5.68	0.02
DF1_0.8K	VF4, VF6	None	4	565.35	7.37	0.01
None	VF4, VF6	None	3	569.75	7.49	0.01

Note: K = number of parameters, including constant and error terms; RSS = residual sum of squares; w$_i$ = Akaike's weight, indicating probability of model given the data (Burnham and Anderson 2002).

Table 35. Top multiple logistic regression models (ΔAICc <4.0) describing the relationships between the probability of an inaccessible Ferruginous Hawk nest cluster being successful in a given year and various oil and gas development factors (DFs), landcover/vegetation factors (VFs), climatic variables, and interactions and in the Rawlins, Wyoming study area.

Development Factors	Vegetation Factors	Climate Variables	Interactions	K	Log(L)	ΔAICc	w_i
DF1_2K	VF3	PDSI	DF1_2K*PDSI	5	-216.47	0.00	0.12
DF1_0.8K	VF3	PDSI	None	4	-217.74	0.51	0.09
DF1_0.8K	VF3	WintPPT	None	4	-217.87	0.78	0.08
DF1_2K	VF6	PDSI	DF1_2K*PDSI	5	-217.17	1.40	0.06
DF1_2K	VF3	PDSI	None	4	-218.39	1.82	0.05
DF1_0.8K	VF6	PDSI	None	4	-218.42	1.88	0.05
DF1_2K	VF3	WintPPT	None	4	-218.53	2.10	0.04
DF1_0.8K	VF2, VF4	PDSI	None	5	-217.86	2.79	0.03
DF1_2K	None	PDSI	DF1_2K*PDSI	4	-218.92	2.88	0.03
DF1_0.8K	VF2, VF4	WintPPT	None	5	-218.01	3.08	0.03
DF2_0.8K	VF3	WintPPT	None	4	-219.03	3.10	0.03
DF1_2K	VF6	PDSI	None	4	-219.04	3.12	0.03
DF2_0.8K	VF3	PDSI	None	4	-219.13	3.30	0.02
DF1_2K	VF6	WintPPT	None	4	-219.16	3.36	0.02
DF1_0.8K	VF3	None	None	3	-220.21	3.44	0.02
DF1_0.8K	VF4	PDSI	None	4	-219.21	3.45	0.02
None	VF3	WintPPT	None	3	-220.23	3.48	0.02
None	VF3	PDSI	None	3	-220.29	3.59	0.02
DF1_0.8K	None	PDSI	None	3	-220.33	3.68	0.02
DF1_0.8K	VF4	WintPPT	None	4	-219.33	3.70	0.02

Note: K = number of parameters, including constant and error terms; Log(L) = log likelihood; w_i = Akaike's weight, indicating probability of model given the data (Burnham and Anderson 2002).

the negative relationship with PDSI, whereas in previous models both variables entered the models together and indicated the same negative association with PDSI but a positive association with WintPPT.

The top six models of productivity at inaccessible nests ($n = 951$) suggested less model variability (Table 36) relative to the previous success and productivity models;

however, the top model still provided only very weak explanatory power (adjusted $R^2 = 7.3\%$). The top models suggested that productivity at inaccessible nests related positively to DF1_0.8K, VF1, and PDSI_lyr, and negatively to DF2 (at either scale), VF3, and WintPPT. The models of success and productivity at inaccessible nests differed considerably, although both showed a positive relationship with OG development within 0.8

Table 36. Top multiple linear regression models (ΔAICc <4.0) describing relationships between productivity per nest attempt at inaccessible Ferruginous Hawk nests in a given year and oil and gas development factors (DFs), landcover/vegetation factors (VFs), and climate variables and in the Rawlins, Wyoming study area.

Development Factors	Vegetation Factors	Climate Variables	Interactions	K	RSS	ΔAICc	w_i
DF1_0.8K, DF2_0.8K	VF1, VF3	PDSI_lyr, WintPPT	DF2_0.8K*VF1	8	1153.55	0.00	0.29
DF1_0.8K, DF2_0.8K	VF1, VF3	WintPPT	DF2_0.8K*VF1	7	1157.41	1.14	0.16
DF1_0.8K, DF2_0.2K	VF1, VF3	PDSI_lyr, WintPPT	DF2_2K*VF1	8	1155.05	1.24	0.15
DF1_0.8K, DF2_0.8K	VF1, VF3	PDSI_lyr, WintPPT	None	7	1158.36	1.92	0.11
DF1_0.8K, DF2_2K	VF1, VF3	WintPPT	DF2_2K*VF1	7	1158.93	2.39	0.09
DF1_0.8K, DF2_0.8K	VF1, VF3	WintPPT	None	6	1162.36	3.16	0.06

Note: K = number of parameters, including constant and error terms; RSS = residual sum of squares; w_i = Akaike's weight, indicating probability of model given the data (Burnham and Anderson 2002).

km, and negative relationships with non-OG roads within 0.8 km, VF3, and WintPPT.

Across all years, nest success was significantly lower at accessible nests (62.5 ± SE of 2.9%) than at inaccessible nests (93.6 ± 0.8%; t = -10.4, df = 326, P < 0.001). Similarly, average productivity across all years was significantly lower at accessible nests (1.61 ± 0.08 nestlings produced per nesting attempt) than inaccessible nests (2.74 ± 0.04; t = -12.2, df =397, P <0.001). These pronounced differences between success and productivity at accessible and inaccessible nests may have swamped any potential relationships with development, vegetation, or climate variables. In other words, accessibility alone appears to have had an overriding influence on success and productivity.

Objective 5: Assess the response of Ferruginous Hawks to artificial nest structures.

Neal (2007) determined that the average number of alternative nests found in Ferruginous Hawk nest clusters

was significantly higher before ANS mitigation began (3.3 ± SE of 0.10 nests per cluster pre-ANS mitigation, 2.1 ± 0.12 nests per cluster post ANS mitigation; t = -7.66, df = 463, P < 0.001). He also found that Ferruginous Hawks at inaccessible nest sites spent more minutes attending, delivered more prey items, made more proximate hunting attempts, and flushed from the nest less often than pairs nesting at sites that were accessible to mammalian predators (Table 37). Additionally, although the data were limited in scope, over the years 21 adult or nestling mammalian-depredation events were recorded in association with natural, accessible nests in the study area, whereas only two such events were recorded at inaccessible nests (in both cases involving dead fledglings found near but not in the nests).

Table 37. Total minutes of nest attendance, total prey deliveries, hunting attempts by location, and number of times adults flushed at inaccessible (n = 35 nests) and accessible (n = 15) Ferruginous Hawk nests in the Rawlins, Wyoming study area from 2000–2004 (from Neal 2007). All values are calculated on a per-nest basis and reflect consistent observation effort (6 hours total) at all nests.

Accessibility Category	Minutes of Nest Attendance	Prey Deliveries	Hunting Attempts by Location				Total Hunting Attempts	# Flushes
			Nest	Perch	Air	Ground		
Inaccessible	194.5	3.1	2.5	0.4	1.0	0.1	4.1	0.1
Accessible	129.5	1.3	0.2	0.5	0.4	0.3	1.5	0.7

Price, Utah Study Area

The results of Objective 1 investigations revealed that the average density of OG wells in proximity to raptor nest clusters increased three to four-fold at the 0.8 and 2.0-km spatial scales during the study period, that the average distance to the nearest well decreased by roughly 20%, and that by 2006 roughly 20% fewer nest clusters had no OG wells within 0.8 and 2.0 km of cluster centroids. That said, as of 2006 still 71% of nest clusters had no wells within 0.8 km and 54% had no wells within 2.0 km.

Golden Eagles

Although compromised by very limited effective sample sizes, the results of Objective 2 investigations suggested that, at least during the period of greatest OG development expansion (1999–2002), used Golden Eagle nest clusters consistently tended to be farther from centers of OG development hotspots than unused clusters; however, this response appeared to fade as the pace of further new development in the hotspot areas subsided after 2002 (Figure 6). This suggests that a high volume of active new well development at least temporarily deterred some Golden Eagles from nesting, but that the presence of established wells and associated maintenance activities did not. Previous studies also suggested that nesting raptors might habituate to repeated disturbance (Andersen et al. 1989, Brown et al. 1999, Steidl and Anthony 2000).

The Objective 3 investigations revealed a distinct negative relationship between overall OG development levels and the probability of Golden Eagle nest clusters being used or active in a given year, whether evaluated at the 0.8 or 2.0-km spatial scale. Further, integrated modeling of vegetation and climate variables illustrated the importance of drought severity in driving activity trends, and that activity patterns varied by habitat. All top use and activity models suggested that Price Golden Eagles responded positively to reduced drought severity. In contrast, previous research in Utah and Idaho suggested that Golden Eagle nest activity was most closely aligned with jackrabbit abundance and distribution (Smith and Murphy 1979, Bates and Moretti 1994, Steenhof et al. 1997), which appear to vary independent of drought conditions (Steenhof et al. 1997). Our results also suggested that cluster activity was higher on the heels of lower-than-average winter precipitation. Mild winter conditions can increase Golden Eagle

reproductive output (Tjernberg 1983), or conversely, severe winters can serve to further reduce reproductive output during periods of reduced prey abundance (Steenhof et al. 1997).

Development-plus model assessments also suggested that the influence of development activities on Golden Eagles varied somewhat depending on habitat. In particular, it appeared that the negative effects of expanding OG development were enhanced in habitats featuring human habitations and increased cover of rabbitbrush and riparian forest (perhaps already marginal nesting and foraging habitats for Price Golden Eagles), whereas expanding development may have had a positive effect in relatively open habitats featuring significant cover of low-growing black sagebrush. Why the latter effect might have occurred is uncertain, but may reflect factors such as development infrastructure providing more hunting perches in otherwise open habitat, possibly development activities leading to a reduction in prevalence of competing mammalian predators in such habitats, or some other positive benefit of development with regard to prey abundance or accessibility in such areas. Because of the potentially large influence of prey on Golden Eagle nesting ecology (e.g., Smith and Murphy 1979, Bates and Moretti 1994, Steenhof et al. 1997), data on prey abundance or habitat associations may have clarified this relationship.

Although again compromised by limited sample sizes due to inconsistent annual monitoring of specific nest clusters, analysis of proportional cluster use and activity histories revealed additional potential insight. The results suggested that the relationship between roads/development and the longer-term activity histories of individual Golden Eagle nest clusters within the study area depended primarily on the diversity of development levels across alternate nests within clusters (i.e., more options) rather than the overall, average levels of development nearby. That is, the development variables that contributed to the models were exclusively "variance" factors, primarily reflecting variation at the more proximate 0.8-km spatial scale in the levels of both OG development and non-OG roads, and always related positively to the probability of eagle nesting activity. In interpreting these results, it is important to recognize that the majority of eagle nest clusters suited to these analyses were located in areas of relatively high development activity, because those were the areas surveyed most regularly and hence a reasonable degree of annual monitoring consistency was achieved. In other words, the available dataset did not effectively represent nest clusters that otherwise would have reflected low development/road variance due to the relative absence of OG development and roads. This may be the reason why the proportional use/activity models did not incorporate average DF1 and DF2 variables and reflect a negative response to overall development levels, as was the case in the analyses of annual cluster use/activity. Had low-development clusters been effectively encompassed, low DF variance could have reflected either uniformly low or high road/development levels, and may not have emerged as a significant predictor of cluster activity in the absence of DF variables reflecting variation in overall road/development levels. Regardless, we reiterate that the discrimination ability of the proportional use/activity models was low, and hence these results, in particular, must be considered with great caution.

Red-tailed Hawks

Compared to Golden Eagles, analyses of relationships for Red-tailed Hawks were much more severely compromised by limited nest-cluster sample sizes. We anticipated this, because we knew from the outset that Golden Eagles were the most common nesters within the study area and that sample sizes for other nesting species would be limited. As with Golden Eagles, inconsistent monitoring histories further limited sample sizes and, because of this, hotspot and proportional use/activity analyses were not possible for Red-tailed Hawks. Moreover, the fact that the annual-use analyses revealed a bewildering array of competing top models (Table 6) compared to the annual activity models (Table 7) may reflect greater difficulty and subjectivity associated with identifying signs of occupation or tending (use), as opposed to actual breeding (active), based on a one-time aerial survey during May. That is, classifying a cluster as active required greater and more concrete evidence than classification as used (see definitions), and as a result, models of cluster use likely contained greater noise. Nevertheless, the two analyses did reveal some consistent patterns and novel, apparent relationships between Red-tailed Hawk nesting activity and development.

The initial development-only analyses of annual cluster use and activity related positively to OG development at the 0.8-km scale, but related negatively to it at the larger scale. Cluster use also related positively to non-OG roads at the smaller scale. That is, these data suggested that the probability of a cluster being used or active was highest in areas with both high OG development and where non-OG roads were relatively prevalent and proximate to nest clusters at the smaller scale, but that these relationships may not hold in the larger landscape and may even reverse for OG development.

Adding vegetation and climate variables suggested additional complexities. Similar to Golden Eagles, climate variables appeared as significant covariates in most of the use models (Table 6) and indicated positive responses to declining drought severity, but a negative response to excessive winter precipitation when the overall drought response was already accounted for. However, no climate variables emerged as significant covariates in the activity models (Table 7), suggesting that actual breeding attempts were not strongly influenced by moisture conditions. As was the case for Golden Eagles, both the use and activity models also typically included one or more vegetation factors, suggesting that the probability of cluster activity varied by habitat. In particular, VF2 figured prominently in models for both species and consistently indicated higher activity levels in habitats featuring relatively high cover of mountain and basin big sagebrush, and lower activity in habitats dominated by mixes of pinyon, juniper, and mixed-species sagebrush.

In the presence of VF and climate variables, the top use and activity models also revealed a mixed relationship with DF1; i.e., a positive relationship at the 0.8-km scale but a negative relationship at the 2.0-km scale. The apparently conflicting results for the two DF1 variables appear to suggest that Red-tailed Hawks benefited from a degree of proximate development activity, perhaps resulting from creation of more open habitat, increasing prey availability, or providing new hunting perches that render prey more accessible. Janes (1984) found that Red-tailed Hawk reproductive success correlated more strongly with the distribution and density of hunting perches than with actual prey abundance. That is, prey accessibility may be more important than actual abundance. The full use models also suggested a positive influence of non-OG roads within 0.8 km. Therefore, both the development-only and development-plus use and activity models indicated positive associations with proximate OG development and non-OG roads. The Red-tailed Hawk is an abundant, widespread raptor species (Preston and Beane 1993) and apparently tolerant of human activity (Andersen et al. 1989). For example, Red-tailed Hawk productivity in Wisconsin was positively associated with urban density and area of roads (Stout et al. 2006). In contrast to these findings, however, our results suggested that OG development had a negative influence on cluster use and activity at the larger spatial scale (2.0 km), perhaps reflecting a saturation threshold at this broader spatial extent. The activity model also uniquely included a significant interaction between DF1_0.8K and VF3, suggesting that the positive effect of increasing, proximate development activity on the probability of a nest being active in May was muted in habitats dominated by mixes of riparian forest, grass, forbs, and/or oak-maple. The latter may provide further support for the notion that the positive response to proximate development occurs in part because OG infrastructure provides additional hunting perches and access to prey in the predominant pinyon-juniper habitats of the Price study area. Riparian-forest habitats interspersed with open grass/forb patches may already provide ideal combinations of suitable hunting perches, open hunting areas, and accessible prey for Red-tailed Hawks, such that further development may compromise rather than enhance the value of such habitats.

Prairie Falcons

Even more so than for Red-tailed Hawks, small sample sizes due to limited nesting habitat and inconsistent monitoring histories, as well difficulties associated with monitoring cavity nests from the air, greatly limited the utility of available data for Prairie Falcons. An additional limitation that applied to this species was that we did not evaluate potential interactions in the annual use and activity models due to the real danger of spurious results from model overfitting when the ratio of potential predictors to sample units is excessive.

Unlike for both Golden Eagles and Red-tailed Hawks, the initial development-only analyses of annual cluster use and activity revealed no significant relationships for Prairie Falcons. Similar to both other species, however, once vegetation and climate variables were included, significant models and development relationships emerged. Similar to Red-tailed Hawks, and despite a limited difference in the numbers of nesting events classified as used ($n = 34$) and active ($n = 28$), the Prairie Falcon annual-use analysis revealed a much more complex array of top models than the annual-activity analysis (Tables 8 and 9). Nevertheless, again some common overarching patterns were evident. Similar to the other species, various VFs figured into most models, indicating variable responses depending on habitat. In this case, negative relationships between cluster use or activity and VF3 and VF4 were apparent in all top use and activity models, indicating negative responses to habitats featuring relatively high cover of riparian forest, grass, forbs, and black sagebrush or pinyon, pinyon-juniper mix, and barren lands, and positive responses to desert shrub and agricultural habitats. All use and activity models also suggested a positive response to decreasing drought severity, but a negative response to excessive winter precipitation with the overall drought effect already accounted for. In southern Idaho, drought severity influenced ground squirrel (*Spermophilus* spp.) population fluctuations, which in turn influenced Prairie

Falcon reproductive rates (Steenhof et al. 1999). In contrast, excessive winter precipitation may limit prey availability prior to the start of the nesting season. For example, a spring snowstorm in northern Wyoming correlated with reduced abundance of avian prey and nesting cessation in Prairie Falcons (Squires et al. 1991) and high precipitation levels before and during the breeding season reduced productivity per nest start in Idaho (Steenhof et al. 1999).

Top models suggested that Prairie Falcon cluster use had a mixed relationship with DF1 when both scales were included in the same model (i.e., use related positively to OG development at both scales, when considered individually, but related negatively to OG development at the 2.0-km scales when considered simultaneously). This may suggest that a degree of proximate OG development may have been beneficial to Prairie Falcons, but not if the level of OG activity was too great at the broader 2-km scale. In the Price study area, dominated by pinyon-juniper vegetation, OG development may benefit Prairie Falcons by creating open foraging areas required by breeding birds (Squires et al. 1993). Prairie Falcons in Wyoming ($n = 6$) foraged in areas with a greater density of wells; however, these areas were also relatively close to the aerie and had greater cover of grasslands, revealing the potential for confounding between well density and optimal foraging habitat (Squires et al. 1993). Cluster use in Price also related negatively to non-OG development at both spatial scales. Although cluster activity also related negatively to non-OG development within 0.8 km, the top activity models identified no other significant relationships with development. This suggests that the probability of a Prairie Falcon nest being active in May was most sensitive to the proximity of non-OG roads, perhaps reflecting the fact that many of the miscellaneous non-OG roads in the area are most likely to intrude closely into the low cliff and outcrop areas used by nesting Prairie Falcons. Boyce (1988) found that Prairie Falcon productivity in the Mojave Desert related negatively to the number of nearby roads, as well as reduced foot-travel times to nests.

Common Species Patterns

With respect to development, only Price Golden Eagles exhibited consistent negative relationships with OG development at both the 0.8 and 2.0-km spatial scales. However, hotspot analyses suggested that the negative influence of OG development may have been most pronounced during peak development periods and declined once the birds acclimated to existing development levels. In contrast, Red-tailed Hawks and Prairie Falcons commonly exhibited mixed relationships with OG development; i.e., both species appeared to benefit from a degree of OG development within 0.8-km of nest clusters, but this relationship diminished, or even reversed, when OG development was assessed at the broader 2.0-km spatial scale. Both the top Golden Eagle and Red-tailed Hawk models also suggested positive associations with non-OG roads, although the scales at which we detected these relationships differed. In contrast, non-OG roads influenced Price Prairie Falcons negatively. Top models for both Golden Eagles and Red-tailed Hawks also suggested significant interactions between development and vegetation, but the nature of the relationships differed for each species.

The annual use and activity models for all three species also commonly included one or more significant VFs, indicating that the probability of cluster use and activity varied by habitat. The Golden Eagle and Red-tailed Hawk models most commonly included relationships with VF2, which indicated higher activity levels in habitats featuring relatively high cover of mountain and basin big sagebrush, and lower activity in habitats dominated by mixes of pinyon, juniper, and mixed-species sagebrush. In contrast, the Prairie Falcon models most commonly included relationships with VF3 and VF4, indicating negative responses to habitats featuring relatively high cover of riparian forest, grass, forbs, and black sagebrush or pinyon, pinyon-juniper mix, and barren lands, and positive responses to desert shrub and agricultural habitats.

All three species also exhibited positive relationships to wetter current-year conditions (i.e., reduced drought severity), but negative relationships to pre-nesting season winter precipitation when both variables were considered together. This suggests a general positive effect of wetter conditions, as long as pre-nesting conditions were not overly wet or extreme. The potential negative influences of drought on Prairie Falcons (Steenhof et al. 1999) and winter severity or precipitation on both Golden Eagles (Tjernberg 1983, Steenhof et al. 1997) and Prairie Falcons (Steenhof et al. 1999) have been discussed previously. However, the absence of climate variables as significant covariates in the activity models for Red-tailed Hawks suggested that actual breeding attempts of this species were not affected to the same degree by climatic variability. The dearth of previous research documenting such climatic relationships for Red-tailed-Hawks appears to this conclusion.

Rawlins, Wyoming Study Area

Objective 1 investigations revealed that a substantial increase in OG development occurred in the Rawlins Study area between 1978 and 2006, with the number of active wells nearly tripling during this period. The number of wells within 0.8 and 2.0 km of surveyed nest clusters increased more than five-fold, while the average distance from nest-cluster centroids to the nearest well decreased approximately 20% (Table 12). However, in 2006, 86% of nest clusters still had no wells within 0.8 km and 74% had no wells within 2.0 km (Table 13).

☐o☐☐en ☐☐☐es

Due to limited sample sizes, we were unable to assess effectively changes in the distribution of Golden Eagle nest clusters by status in relation to development (Objective 2). However, initial Objective 3 investigations of development-only relationships suggested that Golden Eagle nesting activity was negatively affected by OG development at both the 0.8 and 2.0-km scales, with a positive relationship with non-OG roads at the 2.0-km scale further suggesting that they benefited from a relatively high prevalence of non-OG roads (typically corresponding to a relatively low prevalence of OG roads and overall development) across the broader landscape surrounding nest clusters.

Integrated modeling of development, vegetation, and climate further suggested that vegetation and climate factors influenced use and activity similarly. Climate appeared to be a particularly important driver of Golden Eagle nesting activity, with all three climate variables present in all top use and activity models. The relationships with climate variables suggested that use and activity were greater during periods of "drought recovery"; i.e., in wetter years, with wetter previous winters (November–February), particularly when following drier years. Jackrabbit numbers may be a major driver of Golden Eagle reproductive output in Utah and Idaho (Smith and Murphy 1979, Bates and Moretti 1994, Steenhof et al. 1997) and appear to cycle independently of climate conditions (Steenhof et al. 1997). However, prairie dogs (*Cynomys* spp.) and ground squirrels may contribute more to the breeding-season diet of Golden Eagles in southern Wyoming (Schmalzried 1976, MacLaren et al. 1988). Cluster use and activity also appeared to relate positively to greater cover of riparian forest, grass, mountain mahogany, and/ or agriculture, and lower cover of relatively high-growing sagebrush species. Ignoring mountain mahogany, this may reflect greater use of and activity in productive bottomland drainage areas (in the arid West, agriculture is commonly associated with these areas).

Although cluster use did not appear to be affected by development after accounting for vegetation and climate influences, there was some indication (i.e., in one of four top models) that cluster activity (i.e., the probability of an actual breeding attempt occurring) was negatively influenced by increasing OG development within 2.0 km. Again, the use models may have contained greater noise due to their reliance on a less rigorous classification scheme. This may have precluded the detection of development relationships in our comparison of annual Golden Eagle nest-cluster use in the Rawlins study area. Investigation of proportional Golden Eagle nest use and activity between 1998 and 2006 revealed more complicated relationships with development. The results suggested that the proportion of years in which Golden Eagle clusters were used or active generally increased in areas with relatively high OG development but low variance in OG development levels, and in areas with high prevalence and variance of non-OG roads. This suggests that proportional use/activity may have been greater in areas of a relatively high OG development and non-OG roads, but only if the degree of change in overall OG development levels was relatively low in the areas around nest clusters (i.e., better if not in areas of rapid development). A similar theme emerged in the Price study-area "hotspot" analysis, suggesting that active nests there tended to be farther from development hotspots during the period of most rapid development. While previous research suggests nesting raptors can habituate to human disturbance (Andersen et al. 1989, Brown et al. 1999, Steidl and Anthony 2000), responses to initial exposure may still be significant. For example, Red-tailed Hawks flushed in response to helicopter over-flights at 53% of previously unexposed nests, compared to only 8% of nests exposed to such activities during the previous year (Andersen et al. 1989).

Proportional Golden Eagle cluster use and activity generally increased with non-OG road coverage and at territories with greater variability in the coverage of non-OG roads. Because the location and cover of non-OG roads was static across years (see methods detailing road classification and addition procedures), the variance detected in this development factor was actually driven entirely by use of alternate nests within clusters (i.e., two widely spaced alternate nests within a given cluster may have been surrounded by substantially different road networks). In this scenario, the positive association between proportional use and activity and variance in non-OG roads may actually reflect greater use and activity within territories containing alternate

nests situated in diverse non-OG road-network settings (i.e., territories providing greater flexibility to Golden Eagles in response to the non-OG road network). The vegetation relationships were somewhat variable between the best proportional use and activity models, but all top models identified a positive association with greater cover of riparian forest, grass, mountain mahogany, and/or agriculture, and lower cover of relatively high-growing sagebrush species.

Ferruginous Hawks

The potential response of Ferruginous Hawks to OG development was complicated by documented Ferruginous Hawk use of OG structures (mostly condensation tanks) for nesting and subsequent mitigation with ANSs. In an attempt to control the potential confounding this situation presented, we first assessed the response of Ferruginous Hawks to OG development by limiting our consideration to nest clusters that did not contain ANSs. However, due to the common use of ANSs for nesting in later years in the Rawlins study area, it was not possible to assess changes in the distribution of nest clusters by breeding status in relation to development (Objective 2) without inclusion of ANS nest clusters. With this caveat in mind, we found that used and active nests were significantly closer to centers of development hotspots relative to unused or other nests. This likely reflected a shift to the use of ANS structures situated within and near development hotspots (i.e., installation of ANS began in 1987 and our hotspot assessment covered the period 1998-2006). A graphical assessment of the density of active Ferruginous Hawk nest clusters pre- and post-ANS installation supported this conclusion (Figure 13).

Non-ANS Relationships.—Considering relationships between non-ANS nest clusters and development alone, Ferruginous Hawk annual cluster use and activity exhibited a mixed relationship with development factors at the 0.8 and 2.0 km scales when the influence of both scales was considered simultaneously. These mixed relationships suggested that nest-cluster use and activity were greater in areas with less OG development and proportionately more non-OG roads nearby (0.8-km scale), but that these relationships diminished with greater distance (2.0-km scale). After accounting for the potential influence of vegetation and climate on annual cluster use and activity, only nest-cluster activity models still revealed a negative relationship with OG development at the 0.8 km scale. The loss of this relationship in models of cluster use may suggest that cluster use (i.e., occupancy, tending, etc.) was less sensitive to OG development compared to actual breeding events, but more likely reflected the effects of greater noise in the use models from a less rigorous classification scheme. Previous research on Ferruginous Hawks and OG development produced mixed results (Harmata 1991, Van Horn 1993, Zelenak and Rotella 1997, Keough 2006). Most strikingly, nest activity in eastern Utah was reportedly greater in association with more OG wells and smaller distances to the nearest well, but productivity was greater farther from wells (Keough 2006). It is important to note that the majority of nests in this study were located in relatively secure junipers, because nest security may decrease the sensitivity of Ferruginous Hawks to human disturbance (Lokemoen and Duebbert 1976, Neal 2007).

Both full use and activity models suggested a positive relationship with non-OG roads at the 0.8-km scale, but a negative relationship with this factor at the 2.0-km scales. Again, this mixed relationship may reflect an initial benefit of roads to nesting Ferruginous Hawks that diminishes or reverses with over-saturation in the broader landscape. A positive association with roads was reported previously for Ferruginous Hawks in Montana, where the density of ground-squirrel burrows was greater along roadsides compared to adjacent grasslands (Zelenak and Rotella 1997). The authors speculated that ground squirrels might have been attracted to roadsides due to the availability of forage vegetation and disturbed soils. Similarly, higher densities of Stephens' kangaroo rats (*Dipodomys stephensi*) on dirt roads in California may have been related to easy access to burrows, forage vegetation, dust bathing, and movement corridors (Brock and Kelt 2004). Zelenak and Rotella (1997) further speculated that increased prey abundance associated with extensive OG road networks might have benefited Ferruginous Hawks in their study.

Variable interactions suggested that the positive relationships between proximate non-OG roads and both non-ANS cluster use and activity were enhanced in habitats featuring more evergreen forest mix, but less Wyoming big sagebrush or agriculture. One might speculate that roads provide openings in forested habitats for this open-country raptor, but this relationship may also reflect a survey bias in such areas (i.e., the very few nests located in forested habitats may be more regularly visited, and activity more easily detected, in areas with a well-developed road network). In contrast, the reduced positive effect of roads in agricultural habitats may reflect the fact that these areas may already contain high densities of Ferruginous Hawk prey, such as ground squirrels (Schmutz 1989, Zelenak and Rotella 1997), and the previously discussed prey-related road benefits may be less important in such areas.

Overall, the models of annual non-ANS Ferruginous Hawk cluster use and activity suggested similar vegetation and climate relationships. As with Golden Eagles, non-ANS Ferruginous Hawk nesting activity was greater in years of drought recovery. Similar to the discussion for Price-area Prairie Falcons, correlations between prey species, such as ground squirrels, and drought may be partially responsible for this relationship. In Idaho, Ferruginous Hawk reproductive output also varied in response to the abundance of ground squirrels (Steenhof and Kochert 1985), which may be a similarly important dietary component for the species in southern Wyoming (MacLaren et al. 1988). The association of Ferruginous Hawk cluster use and activity with a complex of vegetation factors (i.e., five vegetation factors in the best use and activity models) precluded detailed interpretation of the vegetation relationships. This reality may have been partially responsible for the very poor fit of our Ferruginous Hawk top models (i.e., these models may have been overfit due the inclusion of all but one of the available vegetation factors).

Our assessment of proportional non-ANS cluster use or activity between 1998 and 2006 revealed some commonalities with the relationships gleaned from the annual assessments of use and activity. First, proportional use and activity decreased as the amount of OG development increased within 0.8 km, but this relationship reversed at the 2.0 km scale. Similarly, we also detected the previously discussed positive relationship with non-OG roads at the 0.8-km scale, but not the diminishing or reversing relationship at the 2.0-km scale suggested by the annual assessments. Therefore, both the top annual and proportional use and activity models suggested a negative effect of OG development, but a positive effect of non-OG roads on Ferruginous Hawk cluster status at the 0.8-km scale. This agreement between the poor-fitting annual models and better-performing proportional models strengthens our confidence in the identified non-ANS Ferruginous Hawk cluster status and development relationships.

Similar to Rawlins Golden Eagles, Ferruginous Hawk proportional cluster use and activity related positively to increased variance of non-OG roads. Again, this suggests that proportional use and activity were greater at clusters containing alternate nests in differing road matrices (i.e., more nesting options relative to roads). All Ferruginous Hawk proportional use and activity models revealed a positive association with greater cover of riparian forest, grass, mountain mahogany, and/ or agriculture. All but one top model of Ferruginous Hawk annual and proportional use and activity also suggested positive relationships with greater cover of juniper, basin big sagebrush, Wyoming big sagebrush, and/or agriculture, but less cover of evergreen forest. We suggest these relationships were most likely driven by the cover of grass and sagebrush, as Ferruginous Hawks are known to preferentially select these habitats for nesting and foraging (e.g., see reviews in Olendorff 1993, Bechard and Schmutz 1995). In contrast, previous studies suggested mixed relationships between agriculture and nesting Ferruginous Hawks (Howard and Wolfe 1976, Schmutz 1989, Bechard et al. 1990). These conflicting results may be due to a "threshold" relationship with agriculture. For example, Schmutz (1989) found that Ferruginous Hawk nesting densities in Alberta increased as the proportion of cultivation in the landscape surrounding nests increased to 30%, but decreased thereafter. In this light, no Ferruginous Hawk nest cluster in the Rawlins study area had >12% agricultural cover within 2 km, suggesting the potential for nesting birds to benefit from agriculture at this relatively low level.

ANS Relationships.—Most ANSs present in the Rawlins study area were erected to mitigate Ferruginous Hawk use of OG structures for nesting. Nesting attempts on OG structures, typically condensation tanks, often failed following repeated human visitation to the structure. Nests on such structures were commonly relocated to ANSs erected nearby (i.e., within 1 km) and, as a result, the majority of ANSs were located in areas of relatively high OG development. As discussed in the previous section, Ferruginous Hawk nest use and activity shifted markedly after 1989 into development hotspots and areas of ANS availability. To determine if Ferruginous Hawks nesting on ANSs responded differentially to OG development, we separately assessed relationships between ANS nest-cluster activity and development, vegetation, and climate variables.

Assessing relationships between Ferruginous Hawk ANS cluster use/activity and development alone revealed striking contrasts with non-ANS cluster patterns. ANS nest-cluster use and activity related positively to OG development at both spatial scales, whereas non-ANS cluster use and activity related negatively to OG development, with the effect diminishing at greater distance. Moreover, ANS cluster use and activity related negatively to non-OG roads at the 0.8-km scale, but related positively to non-OG roads at the 2.0-km scale when both scales were considered simultaneously, which is the exact opposite of suggested non-ANS cluster/development relationships. This strongly suggests that the nesting ecology of Ferruginous Hawks afforded access to ANSs for nesting differs markedly from that of breeding pairs nesting on primarily natural substrates.

Similar to the non-ANS development-plus models of cluster use and activity, incorporating vegetation and climate variables into ANS models also produced top use models that performed poorly; however, the top ANS model of cluster activity was nearly identical to the top use models and did not fail the goodness-of-fit test. Overall, the full development-plus annual models suggested that Ferruginous Hawk ANS cluster use and activity related positively to OG development at the 0.8-km scale and that the previously outlined relationship with non-OG roads was unchanged. This relationship with development appears to suggest that ANS cluster use and activity were greater in areas with considerable OG development in the immediate vicinity, but with more non-OG roads in the larger surrounding landscape. Again, comparing top models of ANS and non-ANS nest-cluster status suggested opposite relationships with development factors. Potential benefits of proximate OG development at ANS clusters may be associated with access to previously unavailable prey resources (i.e., through the creation of artificial nest opportunities and hunting perches where few existed historically), increased prey abundance associated with OG roads (see the previous discussion of burrowing mammal abundance associated with roads; Zelenak and Rotella 1997, Brock and Kelt 2004), increased road kill due to higher traffic levels, and/or other potential benefits accrued to prey species associated with OG infrastructure and activities (e.g., road culverts may provide shelter for small mammals, disturbed earth associated with well pads may attract burrowing mammals, etc.). Although the potential benefits of OG development that we suggest are intuitive, previous research corroborates only the relationship between burrowing-mammal abundance and roads; hence, further study is needed to clarify other speculative relationships.

Variable interactions suggested that positive relationships between proximate OG development and ANS cluster use and activity were enhanced in habitats with more riparian forest, grass, mountain mahogany, and/or agriculture. Such habitats were relatively rare near ANS clusters, but data inspection suggested that a few clusters with both high OG development and grass cover also experienced very high use and activity. This may reflect the combined benefits of the previously discussed OG prey effects, prime natural foraging habitat (grass-dominated habitats), and secure nest sites. Perhaps most importantly, compared to many natural-substrate nests, all ANSs were inaccessible from the ground and likely provided nesting birds with a sense of security in the face of development activities (Neal 2007). Previous research suggested that Ferruginous Hawks using relatively secure nest sites were more tolerant of human activities and a wider range of land-use practices surrounding nests (Lokemoen and Duebbert 1976, Gilmer and Stewart 1983, Zelenak and Rotella 1997). Nest security may serve to insulate Ferruginous Hawks from potential disturbance and changes in predator abundance that may be associated with OG development. See Neal et al. (2010) for a more detailed discussion of Ferruginous Hawk use of ANSs in the Rawlins study area and the ability of these structures to mitigate potential OG impacts.

Similar to non-ANS clusters, ANS cluster use and activity related positively to greater cover of riparian forest, grass, mountain mahogany, and/or agriculture, as well as greater pre-nesting winter precipitation. In stark contrast with non-ANSs, however, ANS cluster use and activity were greater when current-year drought conditions were more severe. We speculate that drought severity may have benefited Ferruginous Hawks utilizing ANSs through the concentration of potential prey near OG water sources (e.g., evaporation pits). Although we were unable to find published research to support this speculation, it is clear that wildlife commonly become concentrated near water sources in the arid West.

Nesting Success and Productivity.—Our initial objective was to assess differences in Ferruginous Hawk nest success and productivity at a subset of nest clusters to determine the influence of development on reproductive output. Because previous evidence suggested that success and productivity might differ between non-ANS and ANS nests (e.g., Tigner and Call 1996) and we suspected that nest substrate and accessibility also might influence these reproductive parameters, we hoped to describe patterns of nest success and productivity in relation to these nest classifications. However, as discussed in our results, sample sizes limited our comparison to simple categorization of nests as accessible or inaccessible (i.e., to potential ground-based humans and nest predators). The majority of nests classified as accessible were located on natural substrates and included no ANSs, whereas inaccessible nests typically were located on manmade substrates and especially ANSs (i.e., our reduced classification of nests as accessible or inaccessible largely reflected the contrasts between natural and. manmade nesting substrates and non-ANS versus ANS nests).

Overall, assessments of fit indicated very poor performance for models of nesting success and productivity for both accessible and inaccessible nests. This was likely because accessibility alone had the greatest influence on success and productivity, and little additional information could be modeled after separating nests into these groupings. The fact that both nest success

and productivity were significantly lower and more variable at accessible nests supports this conclusion. It may be that success and productivity at accessible nests is more chance driven, due to the vulnerability of such nests to predation. In contrast, inaccessible nests were nearly always successful, and therefore nearly all such nests were at least minimally productive.

Neal's (2007) work evaluating comparative use of alternate nests and nest attendance and foraging relationships at accessible and inaccessible nests provided further insight about how use of ANSs and nest inaccessibility yielded greater success and productivity for Ferruginous Hawks. A significant reduction in the number of alternate nests used within ANS-based nesting territories suggested that birds using ANSs were less dependent on maintaining large suites of alternate nests. Several factors may be involved in this dynamic. For example, increased long-term stability of ANS substrates may allow for greater perennial use of individual nests. In fact, Neal (2007) found that although natural, inaccessible nests were overall the most successful of all nests, and generally were also the most productive, their productivity tended to decline over time, suggesting that nest and substrate deterioration may have been an issue. Another possibility, though purely speculative at present, is that the wire bases of the ANSs may allow for greater annual "flushing" of the nest substrate by rains, thereby reducing the need to rotate nest use to help control build-up of nest parasites (Philips and Dindal 1977). Perhaps most importantly, however, in light of Neal's findings, reduced sensitivity to disturbance from ground-based activities and predators may be the most likely explanation for why reliance on multiple, alternative nests is reduced for breeding pairs using ANSs. Mammalian predators such as coyotes (*Canis latrans*), badgers (*Taxidea taxus*), bobcats (*Lynx rufus*), and foxes (*Vulpes* spp.) are thought to be serious threats to ground-nesting Ferruginous Hawks and recently fledged young (Bechard and Schmutz 1995). Human intrusions also likely function directly and indirectly as predation events through direct persecution of hawks, nest destruction, and the provision of scent trails or roads for other ground predators (L. Apple and J. Tigner personal communication; M. Neal personal observation). The apparent significant benefit of nesting on inaccessible substrates makes perfect sense in light of this evidence. Lokemoen and Duebbert (1976) also suggested that Ferruginous Hawks nesting on relatively secure substrates (i.e., trees) might be less sensitive to human activity compared to ground nesters. Suter and Joness (1981) also suggested that nest security could be an important determinant of raptor responses to human disturbance.

Neal's (2007) nest-attendance and prey-delivery results further clarified the fact that the apparent reduction in sensitivity to ground-based disturbance and depredation potential translated to breeding adults at ANSs and other inaccessible nests being able to dedicate significantly more time to ensuring efficient provisioning and care of their young, which in turn translated to greater overall success and productivity for such nests compared to accessible nests. Schmutz et al. (1984) also found that ANSs were more successful than natural nests (95% vs. 67% of nests reaching near fledging age) for Ferruginous Hawks nesting in Alberta, and concluded that ANSs can be a useful tool for augmenting Ferruginous Hawk nesting in areas where prey are available but natural nest sites are sparse.

Red-tailed Hawks

As with Golden Eagles, small sample sizes precluded Objective 2 assessments for Red-tailed Hawks. Investigation of relationships between development alone and annual cluster use and activity suggested, however, that Red-tailed Hawks responded negatively to overall OG development levels at both the 0.8 and 2.0 km spatial scales. In contrast, cluster activity related positively to non-OG roads at both scales. This relationship with development was similar to that shown for Golden Eagles, and for non-ANS Ferruginous Hawk nest clusters when the influence of either scale was considered alone.

Modeling annual Red-tailed Hawk cluster use and activity in relation to development, vegetation, and climate also revealed that development levels influenced use, but not cluster activity. Red-tailed Hawk cluster use related negatively to OG development at the 0.8-km scale, but related positively at the 2.0-km scale. This suggests that the negative influence of OG development diminished with distance. Additionally, cluster use related negatively to non-OG roads within 2.0 km. The apparent lack of development effects relative to cluster activity, when relationships were detected for cluster use, suggests that actual breeding attempts may have been less sensitive to the effects of development. As previously discussed for Price Red-tailed Hawks, previous research suggested that Red-tailed Hawks are relatively tolerant to human activities and human-dominated landscapes (Andersen et al. 1989, Stout et al. 2006).

The top models of Red-tailed Hawk use and activity suggested that habitat characteristics also were influential (the top models of use and activity each contained four vegetation variables). Similar to Rawlins Golden Eagles and Ferruginous Hawks, Red-tailed Hawks exhibited a positive response to greater cover of riparian forest,

grass, mountain mahogany, and/or agriculture. Riparian forest and agricultural areas (both are commonly found in bottomland areas in of the arid West), in particular, are known to be important nesting and foraging habitats for Red-tailed Hawks in the West (Platt 1971, Bosakowski et al. 1996). Red-tailed Hawks in Rawlins also responded positively to reduced drought severity, and to a lesser extent, wetter pre-nesting winter conditions and drier conditions during the previous year. Again, this suggests an association with drought recovery, a pattern also detected for Rawlins Golden Eagles and non-ANS Ferruginous Hawks.

Prairie Falcons

Similar to the situation for the Price study area, Prairie Falcon sample sizes were most limited among the species evaluated in the Rawlins study area, and precluded Objective 2 "hotspot" assessments. Initial assessments of relationships between Prairie Falcon nest cluster use and activity suggested, however, that both increased OG development levels and high prevalence and proximity of non-OG roads influenced Prairie Falcon nesting negatively. This suggests that Prairie Falcons may have been the most sensitive of the four species assessed in the Rawlins study area to general human activities.

After consideration of the potential influence of vegetation and climate variables, models of annual Prairie Falcon cluster use and activity still suggested a negative relationship with both OG development and non-OG roads, although the scale at which the influence was detected shifted from 0.8 km for use models to 2.0 km for activity models. Again, this suggests that Rawlins Prairie Falcons were the most sensitive to all types of human development. As was discussed for Price Prairie Falcons, roads and accessibility for humans influenced Prairie Falcon productivity in the Mojave Desert negatively (Boyce 1988). In contrast to these results, however, Holthuijzen (1989) did not detect a negative response of nesting Prairie Falcons to road and dam construction within 1.0 km of aeries in Idaho. It is important to note, however, that aeries in the Idaho study were located on cliffs at least 50 m above the sources of potential disturbance, which may have served to insulate them from disturbance. In comparison, most eyries in the Rawlins study area were located on low cliffs and outcrops, much more proximate to ground-based activities. The ability of nest height to influence disturbance responses has been demonstrated for nesting Bald Eagles in relation to pedestrian traffic (Watson 2004).

A consistent development x vegetation interaction in the use and activity models further suggested that the negative influence of OG development was enhanced in habitats featuring relatively high cover of barren land, but diminished in habitats with relatively high cover of Wyoming big sagebrush. Prairie Falcons foraging during the breeding season may prefer open grassy and barren habitats, and given their inherent openness, OG development may be unlikely to confer any further advantages to Prairie Falcons in such habitats. In contrast, openings created in sagebrush habitats by roads, well pads, and pipelines may provide potential benefits (e.g., see our previous discussions about burrowing mammal associations with roads) that serve to diminish the general negative impacts of OG activities for nesting Prairie Falcons in the Rawlins study area.

In regards to vegetation and climate, both the use and activity models suggested similar relationships. Prairie Falcon cluster use and activity related positively to VF2, similar to the other Rawlins raptor species, and to wetter winter conditions. To a lesser extent, use and activity also related positively to wetter current-year conditions but drier previous-year conditions (i.e., a drought-recovery pattern). As previously discussed in Price, reduced drought conditions may influence Prairie Falcon nesting indirectly through its influence on prey populations and especially ground squirrels (Steenhof et al. 1999).

Common Species Patterns

Except for ANS Ferruginous Hawks, top use and/or activity models suggested negative relationships with OG development for all four species, although the scale of detection varied. Our results suggest that, among the four species, Prairie Falcons may have been the most sensitive to human activity, with both the use and activity models suggesting negative relationships with both OG development and non-OG roads. Top use and activity models also suggested that Rawlins-area non-ANS Ferruginous Hawks, Red-tailed Hawks, and Prairie Falcons commonly exhibited negative relationships with non-OG roads at the 2.0-km scale. Only the status of non-ANS Ferruginous Hawk clusters related positively to non-OG roads, and this occurred at the smaller spatial scale. Interactions with vegetation appeared to influence the effects of development on cluster use or activity for all but Golden Eagles. Proportional use and activity of both Golden Eagle and non-ANS Ferruginous Hawks related positively to the variance in non-OG roads, suggesting greater utilization of clusters with more variable non-OG conditions at alternate nests (i.e., clusters with more nesting options in relation to non-OG road networks).

Although the vegetation relationships were varied and complex for individual species, all exhibited positive relationships with VF2, suggesting that all benefited to some degree from availability of riparian forest, grass cover, mountain mahogany, and/or agricultural habitats in the surrounding landscape. We speculate that this likely reflects positive associations with productive bottomland or drainage areas and open grassland/hayfield/pasture habitats.

Golden Eagle, non-ANS Ferruginous Hawk, Red-tailed Hawk, and Prairie Falcon use and activity models also suggested common positive relationships with wetter conditions during the corresponding nesting season and greater winter precipitation prior to the nesting season. In addition, for each species either use or activity models (or both) suggested positive relationships with drier conditions the previous year, when the benefit of higher current year and preceding winter moisture also was accounted for. Considered together, these data suggest that raptor nesting activity generally increased during periods of drought recovery. As we have discussed previously, drought conditions may influence fluctuations in ground squirrel populations (Steenhof et al. 1999). Ground squirrels are an important prey item for Prairie Falcons, Ferruginous Hawks, and Red-tailed Hawks in southern Wyoming (MacLaren et al. 1988).

Comparison of Price and Rawlins Results

Both the Price and Rawlins study areas experienced considerable OG development during the study period. The study areas differ some in terms of general landscape features (i.e., primarily pinyon-juniper dominated canyonlands in Price versus sagebrush and grassland-dominated shrubsteppe in Rawlins), histories of development (more protracted in Rawlins), and general patterns of OG development (generally expanded from distinct centers of activity in Price, but was more dispersed in Rawlins during the early years with subsequent activity generally occurring within the existing development landscape). Despite these differences, we were able to explain much of the variance (i.e., 55–58%) associated with patterns of development in the two areas (as measured by a number of road and well type, distance, and density metrics) around relevant raptor nest clusters with relatively simple PCA ordinations that were highly comparable for the two study areas at both the 0.8 and 2.0-km radius scales. This greatly facilitated comparative evaluations of potential development effects across the two study areas.

A comparison of the distribution of used and unused nest clusters relative to centers of significant OG development activity suggested that used Golden Eagle clusters in the Price study area were found farther from development centers during years of peak OG activity. In contrast, Rawlins Ferruginous Hawk cluster use and activity apparently shifted closer to development centers. However, as illustrated in Figure 13, the latter relationship was driven by the shift of nesting activity onto ANSs erected within development areas. Unfortunately, the limited number of nest clusters with adequate survey histories to assess true changes in the distribution of cluster activity prohibited our assessment of other raptor species in this manner.

Modeling annual use and activity patterns of nesting raptors commonly suggested that OG and other human development patterns (i.e., non-OG roads) significantly influenced breeding activity in both study areas. Relationships were still evident after incorporating the influence of vegetation and climate variables. A comparison of the results obtained in the Price and Rawlins study areas suggests a number of common trends, but also reveals some distinct differences. Table 38 provides a comprehensive summary of the results suggested by the top development-only and development-plus models of annual cluster use and activity for both the Price and Rawlins study areas.

Overall, we detected more consistent evidence of potential negative impacts of OG development in the Rawlins study area. Our assessment of nest-cluster use and activity across all years (1978–2006) suggested that all four species of interest (non-ANS Ferruginous Hawks only) exhibited negative relationships with OG development based on top models of use, activity, or both. In contrast, only Golden Eagles demonstrated a consistent negative relationship between annual cluster use or activity and OG development in the Price study area. That said, although Price Red-tailed Hawks exhibited a positive relationship with OG development at the most proximate spatial scale (0.8-km), a negative influence was exhibited at the larger 2.0-km scale, suggesting that too much development in the broader landscape did have a negative influence on this species as well. In comparison, Red-tailed Hawks in the Rawlins study area appeared to show the opposite relationship (i.e., a negative influence at the smaller scale, but that reversed at the larger scale). Our results also appeared to suggest that Rawlins Prairie Falcons demonstrated the greatest sensitivity to both OG development and non-OG road levels surrounding clusters. In contrast, in the Price study area, similar to Red-tailed Hawks, the Prairie Falcon use models suggested a positive relationship to OG development activity proximate to nest clusters (0.8-km scale); however, this relationship was not evident in the models

pertaining to confirmed breeding attempts. Moreover, as was the case in Rawlins, the Price data also indicated a negative relationship between Prairie Falcon nesting activity and the prevalence of non-OG roads, potentially suggesting a consistently higher likelihood of disturbance for this species when exposed to backcountry roads that closely intrude within the low cliff and rock-outcrop nesting habitats preferred by this species. That said, we caution that Price Prairie Falcons were represented in the annual use and activity models by much smaller sample sizes relative to Rawlins Prairie Falcons ($n = 73$ vs. 455), which may have compromised the Price results and led to a higher probability of spurious results. Additionally, assessing nest use (i.e., occupancy or tending) for a pothole nesting species such as the Prairie Falcon may be particularly subjective, especially when derived from limited aerial surveys, further warranting for greater caution in interpreting results for this species.

An assessment of proportional use and activity at specific nest clusters over multiple years also revealed consistent relationships with development. All top proportional use and activity models from both study areas (i.e., Price Golden Eagles and Rawlins Golden Eagles and non-ANS Ferruginous Hawks) suggested positive associations with diversity (i.e., variance) of non-OG roads within 0.8 km of nest clusters. This suggests that at least Golden Eagles and non-ANS Ferruginous Hawks benefit from having a higher diversity of nesting options within their territories in relation to the proximity and density of non-OG roads.

Another distinct similarity in the results from the two study areas is consistent indications of benefit from at least current-year reductions in drought severity. Virtually all models of annual use and activity indicated clear negative responses to increasing current-year drought severity for all species, with the conspicuous exception of Ferruginous Hawks nesting on ANSs in the Rawlins study area. That said, there were other subtler species- and study-area-specific differences. For example, in the Price study area, the negative responses of all species to increased drought severity applied to both current and previous year conditions; however, in many cases, with the PDSI relationships accounted for, a negative relationship with winter precipitation was indicated. In contrast, in the Rawlins study area, in most cases the results suggested a "preference" for wetter current-year conditions, including good winter precipitation, but drier previous-year conditions. However, closer examination of long-term patterns of nesting activity in the Rawlins area in relation to annual moisture conditions suggested that the dominant pattern there was significant drops in activity following very wet years, rather than significant increases in activity

Summary comparison of logistic regression results for top development-only and development-plus (including climate and vegetation covariates) models of annual nest-cluster "use" and "activity" in the Price, Utah, and Rawlins, Wyoming, study areas.

Study Area	Species	# Nesting Events	Dependent Variable[1]	# Top Models[2]	Development-Only Models[3] 0.8 km DF1	DF2	2.0 km DF1	DF2	Development-Plus Models[3] 0.8 km DF1	DF2	2.0 km DF1	DF2	Variable(s) In Model[3] V	C	I
Price	Golden Eagle	1103	Used/Unused	6	−		−	+	−		−	+	X	X	X
			Active/Other	4	−	+		+	−		−	+	X	X	X
	Red-tailed Hawk	217	Used/Unused	18	+	+	−		+		−		X	X	
			Active/Other	1	+		−		+		−		X		X
	Prairie Falcon	73	Used/Unused	13					+		+/−	−	X	X	na
			Active/Other	3						−		−	X	X	na
Rawlins	Golden Eagle	1313	Used/Unused	4	−		−	+					X	X	
			Active/Other	4	−	+	−	+			−		X	X	
	Ferruginous Hawk (non-ANS)	2269	Used/Unused	6	−	+	−/+	+/−		+			X	X	X
			Active/Other	6	−	+	−/+	+/−	−	+			X	X	X
	Ferruginous Hawk (ANS)	1457	Used/Unused	4	+	−	+	+	+			+	X	X	X
			Active/Other	3	+	−	+	+	+			+	X	X	X
	Red-tailed Hawk	584	Used/Unused	14	−		−		−	−	+		X	X	X
			Active/Other	4	−	+	−	+	−	−		−	X	X	X
	Prairie Falcon	455	Used/Unused	10	−	−	−	−	−	−	−	−	X	X	X
			Active/Other	4	−	−	−	+	−	−	−	−	X	X	X

[1] Used = evidence of recent nest tending, occupation, or actual breeding attempt obtained; Unused = no such evidence obtained, despite nest check. Active = breeding attempt confirmed; Other = all other cases, including some used (i.e., evidence of tending, but not actual breeding) and all unused classifications.

[2] As suggested by AIC model selection; i.e., $\Delta AICc < 4.0$.

[3] DF1 represents component one derived from Principal Components Analysis (PCA) and represents overall oil and gas (OG) development levels evaluated within 0.8 km or 2.0 km radii of raptor nest clusters. DF2 represents component two from the PCA and represents the extent and proximity of non-OG roads evaluated at the two spatial scales. +/− indicates a significant ($P \leq 0.15$) contribution to the model and either a positive or negative association with the dependent variable.

[4] "X" denotes that vegetation (V), climate (C), and/or interaction (I) terms were included in at least one top model. "na" = not applicable due to modeling limitations associated with small samples sizes.

following the return of high moisture levels after dry years. Although the reasons for these relationships and differences across the two study areas are unclear, it probably has to do with differences in the overall landscape characteristics of the two study areas. For example, topographic diversity is generally higher in the Price survey area, and portions of the landscape occupied by nesting raptors extend into higher elevations where winter snow cover is more prevalent, but it is also farther south and therefore a somewhat drier landscape overall than in the Rawlins area. These factors may make the Price landscape and its inhabitants generally more sensitive to drought, and may also provide a greater diversity of foraging opportunities under diverse snow-cover conditions, but also may render raptors that nest in the higher elevation areas more sensitive to the vagaries of heavy snow cover. Conversely, due to the generally flatter terrain in the Rawlins area and generally harsher winter conditions, heavy snow cover that lingers well into spring may impede early nesting activities more than in the Price area by both rendering a marginal thermal environment and impeding access to prey necessary for maintaining sufficient early-season body condition for egg laying. That said, one other possibility is that the evaluation of climate relationships in Rawlins encompassed a period of nearly three decades, whereas the Price models encompassed less than one decade. Hence, it may well be that the increased nesting-event samples sizes and modeling of longer-term dynamics in Rawlins simply produced more robust and accurate inference.

Conclusions and Management Implications

A number of past studies investigating the relationship between raptors and human landscapes have failed to account for the potentially confounding influence of vegetation and climate (e.g., Craighead and Mindell 1981, Bechard et al. 1990, Bosakowski et al. 1993, Berry et al. 1998). We found that apparent relationships with development were often modified by modeling of climate and landcover/vegetation variables, further pointing to the importance of considering such in evaluating disturbance effects. That said, our analyses may well have pointed to even greater influences of climatic variation had we been able to model, for example, precipitation patterns at finer spatial and perhaps temporal scales. Additionally, we must reiterate again that our analyses may have suffered markedly from not being able to model information about prey distribution and abundance, known to be another major driver of raptor population dynamics.

Given the retrospective nature of this study, significant limitations of the available raptor monitoring data (discussed further in Smith et al. [2010]), and our limited ability to reflect other potentially important sources of environmental variation (e.g., prey availability), it must be noted that all results derived from this investigation serve only to reveal potential correlations between OG development and raptor nesting activities; i.e., cause-effect inferences cannot be assumed. We have made every effort to clearly identify and address the weaknesses associated with the data available to us. For example, throughout the analyses we adopted a dual cluster-status classification scheme (i.e., used vs. unused and active vs. other). Although this scheme does not conform to recommended standard nest-status terminology, we adopted this approach in an effort to strike a balance between maximum "positive" (i.e., used or active) classification sample sizes and minimum "false positive" classifications. Additionally, we regularly highlight when there was or was not agreement between the results produced by the two different classification schemes, as well as when results suggested poor model fit or low explanatory ability. However, we believe the scope and pace of OG development in the western U.S. clearly points to the critical need for the type of assessment we have performed and point out that datasets better suited to this task do not currently exist and are unlikely to be forthcoming in the near future.

With that said, our results consistently pointed to negative effects of OG development in both study areas for the species with the largest available sample sizes. That is, Price Golden Eagles and Rawlins Golden Eagles and non-ANS Ferruginous Hawks exhibited negative relationships with OG development, even after accounting for the potential confounding influence of vegetation and climate. Only ANS-associated Ferruginous Hawks exhibited consistent positive relationships between cluster status and OG development (Ferruginous Hawk use of ANSs is a special situation; i.e., ANSs were erected to mitigate their attempts to nest on OG structures and is discussed more extensively in Neal et al. [2010]). Additionally, our results suggest that the currently applied nesting-season protection buffers of 0.8-km radius in the Price and Rawlins study areas should not be reduced, as Price-area Golden Eagles and Rawlins-area Ferruginous Hawks, Red-tailed Hawks, and Prairie Falcons exhibited negative relationships with OG development that occurred within 0.8 km of nest clusters. Further, our results suggest that current protections may have been insufficient to preclude negative impacts for all species, as we detected negative relationships between OG development and Price-area Golden Eagles and Rawlins-area Golden Eagles and Prairie Falcons at the broader 2.0-km spatial scale.

An important caveat to consider, however, is that we generally had only insufficient or incomplete monitoring data to work with, primarily because of different initial monitoring objectives and inconsistent surveys, which precluded rigorous evaluation of the long-term trends in nesting densities, nest success, and productivity. Therefore, we were unable to effectively evaluate overall long-term trends in nesting activity in relation to changing development levels, and thus could not determine whether or not the apparent negative effects of development caused significant population-level effects.

To overcome the difficulties HWI encountered during this research and to gain greater insight into appropriate nest-protection guidelines would require that federal land managers employ more rigorous and standardized nest-monitoring protocols in the future. Toward this end, HWI prepared a separate document entitled "*Recommendations for Improved Raptor Nest Monitoring in Association with Oil and Gas Development Activities*" (Smith et al. 2010). This document outlines the data limitations HWI encountered and, even more importantly, provides detailed recommendations for land managers to consider to improve raptor-monitoring efforts in areas experiencing or expected to experience OG development. Adoption of the methods detailed by HWI would not only serve to immediately aid land managers in the protection of raptor nests and nesting activities, but would also contribute to a greater understanding of the disturbance effects of OG development and generate additional data that could be used to more rigorously assess the efficacy of particular spatial and temporal nest protections in the future.

Agresti, A. 1990. Categorical data analysis. John Wiley and Sons, Inc., New York, NY U.S.A.

Andersen, D. E., O. J. Rongstad, and W. R. Mytton. 1986. The behavioral response of a Red-tailed Hawk to military training activity. Raptor Research 20:65–68

Andersen, D. E., O. J. Rongstad, and W. R. Mytton. 1989. Response of nesting Red-tailed Hawks to helicopter overflights. Condor 91:296–299.

Avian Power Line Interaction Committee (APLIC). 2006. Suggested practices for avian protection on power lines: the state of the art in 2006. Edison Electric Institute, APLIC, and the California Energy Commission, Washington, DC and Sacramento, CA U.S.A.

Bates, J. W., and M. O. Moretti. 1994. Golden Eagle (*Aquila chrysaetos*) population ecology in eastern Utah. Great Basin Naturalist 54:248–255.

Bautista, L. M., J. T. Garcia, R. G. Calmaestra, C. Palacin, C. A. Martin, M. B. Morales, R. Bonal, and J. Vinuela. 2004. Effect of weekend road traffic on use of space by raptors. Conservation Biology 18:726–732.

Bechard, M. J, and J. K. Schmutz. 1995. Ferruginous Hawk (*Buteo regalis*). No 172 *in* A. Poole and F. Gill (Editors), The birds of North America. The Academy of Natural Sciences, Philadelphia, PA U.S.A., and The American Ornithologists' Union, Washington, DC U.S.A.

Bechard, M. J., R. L. Knight, D. G. Smith, and R. E. Fitzner. 1990. Nest sites and habitats of sympatric hawks (*Buteo spp.*) in Washington. Journal of Field Ornithology 61:159–170.

Berry, M. E., C. E. Bock, S. L. Haire. 1998. Abundance of diurnal raptors on open space grasslands in an urbanized landscape. Condor 100:601–608.

Blaisdell, J. P., R. B. Murry, and E. D. McArthur. 1982. Managing intermountain rangelands-sagebrush-grass ranges. General Technical Report INT-134. USDA Forest Service, Intermountain Research Station, Ogden, UT U.S.A.

Bosakowski, T., R. D. Ramsey, and D. G. Smith. 1996. Habitat and spatial relationships of nesting Swainson's Hawks (*Buteo swainsoni*) and Red-tailed Hawks (*B. jamaicensis*) in northern Utah. Great Basin Naturalist 56:341–347.

Bosakowski, T., R. Speiser, D. G. Smith, and L. J. Niles. 1993. Loss of Cooper's Hawk nesting habitat to suburban development: inadequate protection for a state-endangered species. Journal of Raptor Research 27:26–30.

Boyce, D. A. 1988. Factors affecting Prairie Falcon fledgling productivity in the Mojave Desert, California. Pages 237–248 *in* R. L. Glinski, B. G. Pendleton, M. B. Moss, M. N. LeFranc, Jr., B. A. Millsap, and S. W. Hoffman (Editors), Proceedings of the Southwest Raptor Management Symposium and Workshop. National Wildlife Federation, Washington, DC U.S.A.

Brambilla, M., D. Rubolini, and F. Guidali. 2004. Rock climbing and raven *Corvus corax* occurrence depress breeding success of cliff-nesting peregrines *Falco peregrinus*. Ardeola 51:425–430.

Brock, R. E., and D. A. Kelt. 2004. Influence of roads on the endangered Stephens' kangaroo rat (*Dipodomys stephensi*): are dirt and gravel roads different? Biological Conservation 118:633–640.

Brown, B. T., G. S. Mills, C. Powels, W. A. Russell, G. D. Therres, and J. J. Pottie. 1999. The influence of weapons-testing noise on Bald Eagle behavior. Journal of Raptor Research 33:227–232.

Bureau of Land Management. 1990. Record of decision and approved resource management plan for the Great Divide Resource Area. USDI Bureau of Land Management, Rawlins Field Office, Rawlins, WY U.S.A.

Bureau of Land Management. 1997. Final environmental impact statement and record of decision, Price coalbed methane project. USDI Bureau of Land Management, Price Field Office, Price, UT U.S.A.

Bureau of Land Management. 2005. U. S. Department of the Interior public land statistics 2005. On-line at http://www.blm.gov/natacq/pls05. Last accessed 18 July 2006.

Burnham, K. P., and D. R. Anderson. 2002. Model selection and inference: a practical information–theoretic approach. Second edition. Springer-Verlag, New York, NY U.S.A.

Craighead, F. C., Jr., and D. P. Mindell. 1981. Nesting raptors in western Wyoming, 1947 and 1975. Journal of Wildlife Management 45:865–872.

Driese, K. L., and N. Nibbelink. 2005. The SE Wyoming cumulative impacts project. Final Report to the Wyoming Game and Fish Department, Cheyenne, WY U.S.A.

Fletcher, R. J., Jr., S. T. McKinney, and C. E. Bock. 1999. Effects of recreational trails on wintering diurnal raptors along riparian corridors in Colorado grassland. Journal of Raptor Research 33:233–239.

Gilmer, D. S., and R. E. Stewart. 1983. Ferruginous Hawk populations and habitat use in North Dakota. Journal of Wildlife Management 47:146–157.

Grubb, T. G., and R. M. King. 1991. Assessing human disturbance of breeding Bald Eagles with classification tree models. Journal of Wildlife Management 55:500–511.

Grubb, T. G., W. W. Bowerman, J. P. Giesy, and G. A. Dawson. 1992. Responses of breeding Bald Eagles, *Haliaeetus leucocephalus*, to human activities in northcentral Michigan. The Canadian Field Naturalist 106:443–453.

Harmata, A. R. 1991. Impacts of oil and gas development on raptors associated with Kevin Rim, Montana. Unpublished report prepared for the USDI Bureau of Land Management, Great Falls Resource Area, Montana. Kevin Rim Raptor Study Group, Biology Department, Montana State University, Bozeman, MT U.S.A.

Holthuijzen, A. M. A. 1989. Behavior and productivity of nesting Prairie Falcons in relation to construction activities at Swan Falls Dam. Final Report. Idaho Power Company, Boise, ID U.S.A.

Hosmer, D. W., and S. Lemeshow. 1989. Applied logistic regression. John Wiley and Sons, Inc., New York, NY U.S.A.

Howard, R. P., and M. L. Wolfe. 1976. Range improvement practices and Ferruginous Hawks. Journal of Range Management 29:33–37.

Janes, S. W. 1984. Influences of territory composition and interspecific competition on Red-tailed Hawk reproductive success. Ecology 65:862–870.

Jongman, R. H. G., C. J. F. ter Braak, and O. F. R. van Tongeren (Editors). 1987. Data analysis in community and landscape ecology. Centre for Agricultural Publishing and Documentation (Pudoc), Wageningen, The Netherlands.

Keough, H. L. 2006. Factors influencing breeding Ferruginous Hawks (*Buteo regalis*) in the Uintah Basin, Utah. Ph.D. Dissertation, Utah State University, Logan, UT U.S.A.

Knick, S. T., and D. L. Dyer. 1997. Distribution of black-tailed jackrabbit habitat determined by GIS in southwestern Idaho. Journal of Wildlife Management 61:75–86.

Kochert, M. N. 1989. Responses of raptors to livestock grazing in the western United States. Pages 194–203 *in* B. G. Pendleton (Editor). Proceedings of the western raptor management symposium and workshop. National Wildlife Federation, Washington, DC U.S.A.

Kochert, M. N., K. Steenhof, C. L. McIntyre, and E. H. Craig. 2002. Golden Eagle (*Aquila chrysaetos*). No 684 *in* A. Poole and F. Gill (Editors), The birds of North America. The Birds of North America, Inc., Philadelphia, PA U.S.A.

Lokemoen, J. T., and H. F. Duebbert. 1976. Ferruginous Hawk nesting ecology and raptor populations in northern South Dakota. Condor 78:464–470.

MacLaren, P. A., S. H. Anderson, and D. E. Runde. 1988. Food habits and nest characteristics of breeding raptors in southwestern Wyoming. Great Basin Naturalist 48:548–553.

McGahan, J. 1968. Ecology of the Golden Eagle. Auk 85:1–12.

Miller, R. F., T. J. Svejcar, and N. E. West. 1994. Implications of livestock grazing in the intermountain big sagebrush region: plant composition. Pages 101–146 *in* M. Vavra, W. A. Laycock, and R. D. Pieper (Editors), Ecological implications of livestock herbivory in the West. Society for Range Management, Denver, CO U.S.A.

Neal, M. C. 2007. Dynamics associated with Ferruginous Hawk (*Buteo regalis*) nest-site utilization in south-central Wyoming. M.S. Thesis. University of Wyoming, Laramie, WY U.S.A.

Neal, M. C., J. P. Smith, and S. J. Slater. 2010. Artificial nest structures as mitigation for natural-gas development impacts to Ferruginous Hawks (*Buteo regalis*) in south-central Wyoming. Technical Note No. 434. USDI Bureau of Land Management, Utah State Office, Salt Lake City, UT, Wyoming State Office, Cheyenne, WY, and Colorado State Office, Lakewood, CO U.S.A.

National Oceanic and Atmospheric Administration (NOAA). 2007. National climatic data center. On-line at http://www7 ncdc.noaa.gov/CDO/CDODivisionalSelect.jsp#. Last accessed May 2007.

Olendorff, R. R. 1993. Status, biology, and management of Ferruginous Hawks: a review. USDI Bureau of Land Management, Raptor Research and Technical Assistance Center, Boise, ID U.S.A.

Parrish, J. R. 1995. Price coalbed methane project, Carbon and Emery Counties, Utah. Technical report prepared for River Gas of Utah. Avocet Consulting, Avon, UT U.S.A.

Philips, J. R., and D. L. Dindal. 1977. Raptor nests as a habitat for invertebrates: a review. Raptor Research 11:87–96.

Platt, J. B. 1971. A survey of nesting hawks, eagle, falcons and owls in Curlew Valley, Utah. Great Basin Naturalist 31:51–65.

Postovit, H. R., and B. C. Postovit. 1989. Mining and energy development. Pages 167–172 in Proceedings of the Western Raptor Management Symposium and Workshop. National Wildlife Federation, Washington, DC U.S.A.

Preston, C. R., and R. D. Beane. 1993. Red-tailed Hawk (*Buteo jamaicensis*). No 52 in A. Poole and F. Gill (Editors), The birds of North America. The Academy of Natural Sciences, Philadelphia, PA U.S.A., and The American Ornithologists' Union, Washington, DC U.S.A.

Rich, T. D., C. J. Beardmore, H. Berlanga, P. J. Blancher, M. S. W. Bradstreet, G. S. Butcher, D. W. Demarest, E. H. Dunn, W. C. Hunter, E. E. Iñigo-Elias, J. A. Kennedy, A. M. Martell, A. O. Panjabi, D. N. Pashley, K. V. Rosenberg, C. M. Rustay, J. S. Wendt, T. C. Will. 2004. Partners in Flight North American landbird conservation plan. Cornell Lab of Ornithology, Ithaca, NY U.S.A. On-line at http://www.partnersinflight.org/cont_plan/ (VERSION: March 2005).

Richardson, C. T., and C. K. Miller. 1997. Recommendations for protecting raptors from human disturbance: a review. Wildlife Society Bulletin 25:634–638.

Ritchie, R. J. 1991. Effects of oil development on providing nesting opportunities for Gyrfalcons and Rough-legged Hawks in northern Alaska. Condor 93:180–184.

Rodemaker, E. J., and K. L. Driese. 2006. Mapping land cover types using remote sensing, GIS and aerial photography for the SW Wyoming, Pinedale and Green River Wyoming Game and Fish Department regions. Final Report to the Wyoming Game and Fish Department, Cheyenne, WY U.S.A.

Romin, L. A., and J. A. Muck. 2002. Utah Field Office guidelines for raptor protection from human and land use disturbances. USDI Fish and Wildlife Service, Utah Field Office, Salt Lake City, UT U.S.A.

Schmalzried, J. T. 1976. Nesting and food habits of the Golden Eagle on the Laramie Plains. M.S. Thesis. University of Wyoming, Laramie, WY U.S.A.

Schmutz, J. K., R. W. Fyfe, D. A. Moor, and A. R. Smith. 1984. Artificial nests for Ferruginous Hawks and Swainson's Hawks. Journal of Wildlife Management 48:1109–1013.

Schmutz, J. K. 1989. Hawk occupancy of disturbed grasslands in relation to models of habitat selection. Condor 91:362–371.

Smith, D. G., and J. R. Murphy. 1979. Breeding responses of raptors to jackrabbit density in the eastern Great Basin Desert of Utah. Raptor Research 13:1–14.

Smith, J. P., S. J. Slater, and M. C. Neal. 2010. Recommendations for improved raptor nest monitoring in association with oil and gas development activities. Technical Note No. 436. Bureau of Land Management, Utah State Office, Salt Lake City, UT, Wyoming State Office, Cheyenne, WY, and Colorado State Office, Lakewood, CO U.S.A.

Sokal, R. R., and F. J. Rohlf. 1995. Biometry: the principles and practice of statistics in biological research. Third Edition. W. H. Freeman and Company, New York, NY U.S.A.

Squires, J. R., S. H. Anderson, and R. Oakleaf. 1991. Prairie Falcons quit nesting in response to spring snowstorm. Journal of Field Ornithology 62:191–194.

Squires, J. R., S. H. Anderson, and R. Oakleaf. 1993. Home range size and habitat-use patterns of nesting Prairie Falcons near oil developments in northeastern Wyoming. Journal of Field Ornithology 64:1–10.

Steenhof, K., and I. Newton. 2007. Assessing nesting success and productivity. Pages 181–192 in D. M. Bird and K. L. Bildstein (Editors), Raptor research and management techniques. Hancock House Publishers, Surrey, British Columbia, Canada, and Blaine, WA U.S.A.

Steenhof, K., and M. N. Kochert. 1985. Dietary shifts of sympatric buteos during a prey decline. Oecologia 66:6–16.

Steenhof, K., M. N. Kochert, L. B. Carpenter, and R. N. Lehman. 1999. Long-term Prairie Falcon population changes in relation to prey abundance, weather, land uses, and habitat conditions. Condor 101:28–41.

Steenhof, K., M. N. Kochert, and T. L. MacDonald. 1997. Interactive effects of prey and weather on Golden Eagle reproduction. Journal of Animal Ecology 66:350–362.

Steidl, R. J., and R. G. Anthony. 2000. Experimental effects of human activity on breeding Bald Eagles. Ecological Applications 10:258–268.

Stout, W. E., S. A. Temple, and J. M. Papp. 2006. Landscape correlates of reproductive success for an urban-suburban Red-tailed Hawk population. Journal of Wildlife Management 70:989–997.

Suter, G. W., II, and J. L. Joness. 1981. Criteria for Golden Eagle, Ferruginous Hawk, and Prairie Falcon nest site protection. Raptor Research 15:12–18.

Swarthout, E. C., and R. J. Steidl. 2003. Experimental effects of hiking on breeding Mexican Spotted Owls. Conservation Biology 17:307–315.

Swenson, J. E. 1979. Factors affecting status and reproduction of Ospreys in Yellowstone National Park. Journal of Wildlife Management 43:595–601.

Tigner, J. R., and M. W. Call. 1996. Effectiveness of artificial nesting structures for Ferruginous Hawks in Wyoming. Pages 137–144 in D. M. Bird, D. E. Varland, and J. J. Negro (editors). Raptors in Human Landscapes. Academic Press, San Diego, CA U.S.A.

Tjernberg, M. 1983. Prey abundance and reproductive success of the Golden Eagle *Aquila chrysaetos* in Sweden. Holarctic Ecology 6:17–23.

USGS National Gap Analysis Program. 2004. Provisional digital land cover map for the southwestern United States. Version 1.0. RS/GIS Laboratory, College of Natural Resources, Utah State University, Logan, UT U.S.A.

Van Horn, R. C. 1993. A summary of reproductive success and mortality in a disturbed Ferruginous Hawk (*Buteo regalis*) population in northcentral Montana, 1990–1992. Journal of Raptor Research 27:94.

Watson, J. W. 2004. Responses of nesting Bald Eagles to experimental pedestrian activity. Journal of Raptor Research 38:295–304.

White, C. M. and T. L. Thurow. 1985. Reproduction of Ferruginous Hawks exposed to controlled disturbance. Condor 87:14–22.

Zelenak, J. R., and J. J. Rotella. 1997. Nest success and productivity of Ferruginous Hawks in northern Montana. Canadian Journal of Zoology 75:1035–1041.

artificial nest structure (ANS): a manmade structure specifically designed to accommodate a raptor nest; in the context of this study, comprising a sturdy 4-m pole sunk ~1m into the ground, with roughly a 1-m² hardware cloth and wood-framed platform affixed to the top of the pole on which the nest is built, and generally with a lateral crossarm extending to the side of the platform to serve as a perch for the adult birds next to the nest (see Tigner and Call 1996).

breeding attempt: laying of at least one egg, regardless of nest fate

disturbance: any human-caused activity interfering with normal wildlife behavior; in the context of this document, disturbance particularly refers to interference with raptor nesting ecology.

nest cluster: a variable number of clustered, alternative nest sites maintained by an individual breeding pair, which they may tend each year and use in different years for actual nesting. Note that a species-specific nest cluster may include some nests that are variably used by other species

nest or cluster status: dual classification schemes adopted for the purposes of statistical analyses. The overlapping classification schemes allowed the comparison of "used vs. unused" and "active vs.

other" nests/clusters. We defined the categories as follows:

(1) "Used" = evidence of recent nest tending, occupation, or actual breeding attempt obtained

"Unused" = no such evidence obtained, despite nest check

(2) "Active" = breeding attempt confirmed

"Other" = all other cases, including some used (i.e., evidence of tending, but not actual breeding) and all unused classifications

nesting success: classification of a nest as either successful or failed

productivity: the number of nestlings produced to at least 80% of the average fledging age for a given species

successful nest: a nest in which at least one nestling survived to at least 80% of the average fledging age for the relevant species

tended nest: a nest that shows evidence of recent activity, maintenance, or sprucing; i.e., fresh sticks, greenery, bowl-lining materials, or whitewash.

These five documents are an integrated series.

BLM Technical Note 432	Raptor Nesting Near Oil and Gas Development: An Overview of Key Findings and Implications for Management Based on Four Reports by Hawk Watch International
BLM Technical Note 433	An Assessment of the Effects of Oil and Gas Field Activities on Nesting Raptors in the Rawlins, Wyoming and Price, Utah Field Offices of the Bureau of Land Management
BLM Technical Note 434	Artificial Nest Structures as Mitigation for Natural-Gas Development Impacts to Ferruginous Hawks (Buteo regalis) in South-Central Wyoming
BLM Technical Note 435	Accipiter Use of Pinyon–Juniper Habitats for Nesting in Northwestern Colorado
BLM Technical Note 436	Recommendations for Improved Raptor Nest Monitoring in Association with Oil and Gas Development Activities